A GROUN

MW01484067

By
BOBBIE ROSENCRANS, MSW

THE LAST
SECRET

Daughters Sexually Abused
By Mothers

Safer Society Press
PO BOX 340 • BRANDON, VERMONT 05733

EDITORS: Euan Bear and Eileen Murray

DESIGN: Barbara Poeter, Pittsford, VT

TYPESETTING: Amy Rothstein, Pond Productions, Waltham, MA

PRINTING: BookCrafters, Fredericksburg, VA

ORDER FROM:

THE SAFER SOCIETY PRESS
A division of The Safer Society Foundation, Inc.
PO Box 340
Brandon, VT 05733-0340
(802) 247-3132

$20.00
U.S. funds only
Vermont residents, please add sales tax.

ISBN: 1-884444-36-9

The Last Secret:
Daughters Sexually Abused By Mothers

By Bobbie Rosencrans, M.S.W.

About the Author

Bobbie Rosencrans, M.S.W., is a social worker who has conducted professional training nationally and internationally on the topic of mothers as sex offenders. She is currently preparing a related book on psychotherapy with adult survivors of abuse by mothers. Bobbie Rosencrans, whose previous book was *When You're Ready* (as Kathy Evert), is in private practice, plays banjo in a bluegrass band, and was recently named a distinguished alumna of the University of Michigan's School of Social Work. She can be reached at Elan Place #16, 5000 Marsh Road, Okemos, MI 48864.

Dedication

In loving memory of Fay Honey Knopp, her leadership and caring about individuals and our society, and for the example her life gives me.

And for survivors of abuse by mothers, especially for those whose courage and words give this book's data depth and humanness.

Table of Contents

Preface

The compilation of the survey of daughters who were sexually abused by their mothers has been a difficult project. I have been investigating these daughters' pain for some time, and I have had to exert great effort to stay with it. So why do it? For me, the answer is in these words from a survivor of mother/daughter sexual abuse who had spent many mute years in a state mental institution rather than tell how her mother had sexually abused her during childhood:

> Because the world needs to know. There are sisters silent with this and there should be no more silence.
>
> It is real.
>
> It is there.
>
> It happens.
>
> We are victims … we didn't ask for it.
>
> We are sisters — all of us.

I published an account of my sexual abuse by my mother, *When You're Ready*, under the name Kathy Evert and then found myself in a position to learn about other survivors' experiences. Over a period of years, I have had contact with hundreds of adult survivors of sexual abuse by mothers.

As a psychotherapist, I've treated a number of clients who were sexually abused by their mothers. I've seen and felt the relief that comes when someone understands, or when the survivor learns "I'm not the only one."

As a mental health professional and a survivor, I've been pained by the lack of research and writing about female perpetrators. I gathered these data to increase awareness in the professional community that sexual abuse by females and mothers is occurring daily but remains very hidden. I know that at least one of the mothers described by a daughter in this survey has committed suicide.

I am concerned about the lack of mental health treatment for survivors of sexual abuse by mothers and other women. I did this research to learn how this form of sexual abuse is different from abuse by male perpetrators. There is now a growing body of research on this topic, but at the time there was very little. I was guided primarily by the experiences of other survivors as well as my own.

It has not been easy. This research has led me away from many conventional social views of mothers. Like a sledgehammer, it has driven home new truths. I was unprepared for the initial response. I'd hoped to find 30 women willing to do a detailed survey over a period of a year to 18 months. Instead, I received 93 completed surveys in 8 months. For a while, I was buried in a mass of information I thought I'd never sort out.

As the findings emerged from the survey, I began to have unnerving dreams about the daughters of these sexually abusive mothers entering every area of my life. In one dream, there were so many daughters I went to Chicago and bought a bus to get them all moving in the same direction at the same time.

Finally, I had a powerful dream in which through the window of my office, I saw four or five women hanging around my car in the parking lot. At the end of my workday, they all got in my car with me, and all the way to my house they talked about sexually abusive mothers. I found more of these talking daughters in my back yard, cooking in my kitchen, washing dishes, talking while they drank tea at my table, in my living room and den. They were everywhere, all talking about sexual abuse by mothers. I have a hot tub, and it was also full of talking daughters. They were creating a din even in my dream life.

Near the hot tub in the dream was a large bass drum that I placed on its side so the drumhead was facing up, and I took a Native American-style padded drumstick and began to beat out a strong, slow, beat. Suddenly these dream women came together — young, old, poor, wealthy, various races, sizes — and began to sing. They sang in a collective voice of power and strength I'd never heard in women's voices before. I don't know all the details of their song or even the language in which they sang, but I know that together they sent a very powerful message. Their talking and singing absolutely shattered the quiet and isolation of my world.

Some Native American cultures do not permit women to play that kind of a drum collectively. But I think my dream was saying it will take such rule-breaking to get at the truth about female and mother sex offenders. We will never know the truth if we wait for the mothers to tell it. They do not (and perhaps cannot) tell. Even if they wanted to, very little permission in this society is given for women to be so far outside the stereotypes and social rules for women, especially mothers.

I believe we will learn the truth (at this time and in this society) by asking adult survivors. If we want to know what it was like to be a prisoner of war, we will not ask the prison keepers. We'll ask the POWs. If we want to know about mothers who sexually abuse their children, we'll ask the children after they are emotionally secure without their mothers.

So I have stayed with these women, these daughters who insist on telling, and I've tried to keep the beat and learn their song while at the same time I've often felt the hair raised on the back of my neck by the painful, powerful truth they've expressed. I have absolute respect for these respondents' willingness to risk telling their truths. This book is their song and would not be possible without them.

As a result of their powerful voices testifying to their own realities, the numbers became at times less important than the truths about the issues that they raised. I'm sure that will be frustrating for researchers looking for hard data to crunch, but making space for these voices and reflecting on the issues actually serves the purposes of the study better.

A mountain of data was fed into the computer by my friends, graduate students, and other professionals. Many were survivors of various forms of abuse themselves. One, a woman who had suffered horrible spousal abuse, felt that because she was not abused by a woman, she could help. With remarkable patience and determination she recorded every act of sexual, emotional and physical abuse these daughters reported. Her work expressed support and solidarity. She does not know the respondents' identities, but she knows their pain.

This book would not be possible without their 1,000-plus hours of work. There was no grant or money to pay them, and I can only say, "Thank you," and believe it was a labor of love. They were enormously helpful.

The decision has been made to publish the results of this research in two volumes. This first volume will focus on the abuse experiences of the daughters (and a few sons), and the second volume will focus on their treatment experiences and needs, the reasons for the dearth of knowledge about such abuse, and the possible motivations of offending mothers.

I extend a special "Thank you," to Angela Hoogterp, D.O., a psychiatrist, whose support, friendship and medical advice were essential. Connie Simmons, M.S.W., Barb Eagle, M.S.W., and Grace Gibson, Ph.D., were my steady companions during this long project. Their assistance, feedback, friendship and laughter were invaluable. Rodney Mulder, Ph.D., assisted in management of the data, wrote a computer program for the survey, and offered clinical insights. Thanks go to Grand Valley State University for the computer time. Thanks to Nena Sork, M.S.W., and Jodi Brinser, M.S.W., for their help with managing the data. My son, Michael, helped me manage my personal computer and made it perform invaluable functions. Thanks, Mike.

Dr. Inie Byjkerk and Dr. Eliana Gil have helped more than they'll ever know through what they've taught me about healing and therapy. Their influence is like the steel in reinforced concrete. You don't see it directly, but the concrete is much stronger because it's there.

The late Fay Honey Knopp and Euan Bear of Safer Society Press have shown interest in and support for this project when I felt horribly alone, and I will never forget that kindness.

Anita Montero, publisher of *The Healing Woman* newsletter for abuse survivors, has been a supportive, laughing, serious, understanding, compassionate and loyal voice on the telephone who could make me believe I'd make it through this and have my life back.

This work has been personally painful for me, and the daily contact with others' anguish has ripped open my own wounds. After countless months at the computer, I began to experience physical pain where I experienced abuse as a child. I became greatly agitated by the relentlessness of this research.

I work weekly with Kristen Gaumer, a calm and steady massage therapist, to re-heal and re-close old wounds. I am grateful for her patience, skill, kindness and easy laugh while she steadfastly treats me. I can relax with my head in Kris' hands, and Kris has been a witness to my inner pain.

I would be remiss if I did not thank my grandmothers and great aunts. As a child, I was abused by my mother, but I also knew I was loved by my wonderful great aunts who remain my personal models of gentleness, strength, and intelligence. I thank them for their willingness to publicly own what's important in life. They took time to teach me what they knew, and that's important to a child. They also expected me to know what was important and the difference between right and wrong. Through this long process, I've felt them near, and their spirits have guided me.

During my work on this research, my daughter, Kim, gave birth to twins. It is wonderful to see how much she loves these babies.

The research and writing have been humbling experiences. At times, I wanted to stop and reclaim my life. However, the power of the daughters' song has always pulled me back and reminded me that *this is my life song, too.* So I have stayed with their dream song and tried to make it real. They have pushed my limits and made me grow even when I would rather have been shooting baskets in my driveway or going to the beach.

I believe we cannot solve problems we can't articulate or don't fully understand. If this work provides others with a framework to understand and learn, I am satisfied. If it causes others to look further and we learn more, I will be very pleased. If it helps some survivors and offenders to grow and heal, I will be gratified and content. This has been worthwhile for me. I think I've learned some of the daughters' song.

It will be complete.
This song is real.

Late in the day two women sat on a hill
And watched the sun turn golden.
They knew the darkness would come again.
The coolness. The chill and fear.
But they took this moment to reflect.

They were still. And together with the sunset.
The simple beauty and balance of the moment required quiet.
That morning they had each shared their profound truths.
And in this glowing silence,
Watching nature's rhythm
Their minds returned to their earlier words.

Finally one said to the other
"Is it true?"

The second pondered quietly until her answer was ripe.
"Yes."

Part One

THE RESEARCH: CONCEPTS, ASSUMPTIONS, AND PROCEDURE

CHAPTER 1

Concepts and Definitions

any survivors of sexual abuse by mothers feel caught between painful personal experiences and social denial of those experiences.

> It does happen. It hits so deep because this is your main caregiver from birth for most of us. It's hard to realize some of the abuse from a mother because she can hide it so well in the guise of "taking care of you and your health." Because it isn't "penis in the vagina" it may be discounted.

DEFINING SEXUAL ABUSE BY MOTHERS/FEMALES

The survivors of sexual abuse by women often feel betrayed by the "male" aspects of our laws, concepts, and social stereotypes. For most Americans, disengaging male images from sex crimes is like imagining boats without water, a failure to deal with reality that I hope changes as a result of this survey.

To define this abuse properly, we must overcome our own limited thinking. When training professionals, I often note that several points must be reiterated for a valid discussion of sexual abuse by women:

1. **A woman does not have penis.** While this is obvious, it is important to realize that relatively recently a well-known professional wrote that he could not imagine what a woman could do without a penis that was sexually abusive to a child.

2. **A woman can be sexual without a penis.** This is again obvious, but the average American adult knows little about sexual activities between women.

3. **Sexual abuse can occur without a penis.** We are too often unaware that some mothers employ their children for pornographic purposes, insert objects into or orally stimulate a child's genitals, and otherwise behave in sexual ways with children.

4. **To explore sexual abuse by women thoroughly means to explore outside the conventional concepts about women, mothers, sex, mother/child relationships, and heterosexuality.**

5. **The mother perpetrators may have been sexually abused by men and later recreate those abusive dynamics but with themselves as the abusers and their daughters as the victims.** In such instances, we should consider males/penises. However, this is not so-called penis envy, but experience with an abusive male transformed.

These assumptions may seem simplistic, but they are necessary reminders before beginning any serious discussions of mother/female sex offenders.

> [Just] because no penis is involved does not make it "less than"
> male/female incest. Female/female incest feels even crazier to me because
> it can be done in such a way that it can be considered "motherly." People
> "trust" mothers [but] it's just as damaging. Probably even more so. [And]
> the clients are probably less readily able or willing to "confess" than with
> male/female incest.

We need to define sexually abusive acts when committed by a female and/or between two females in the *absence* of male-dominated definitions.

> I feel it is important for the general public to know that mother/daughter
> sexual abuse is not as easily identified as with a male perpetrator. The
> heterosexual view of sexuality limits the ability for people to identify the
> abuse that a woman can perpetrate.

This respondent makes an important point. Some professionals have said, "But what could women do that is sexually abusive to a little girl?" Sexual abuse is sexual abuse, regardless of the perpetrator's gender. We may find it easier to label and even dislike one offender or group of offenders more than another. However, the time has come for brutal honesty about abuse involving females and sex. We also have social systems and professions that influence how we define female- or mother-perpetrated sexual abuse.

LEGAL DEFINITIONS

Our legal system defines specific conditions that must be present to prove sexual abuse has occurred. Legal definitions tend to focus on physical evidence such as semen or pubic hairs, for example. Such evidence does not exist in most of what these daughters identify as female/female sexual abuse. Acts such as oral stimulation of a child's genitals should be considered abuse. Problems arise when investigators do not have enough evidence to charge and convict female perpetrators of child sexual assault. One respondent noted:

> I wish I had physical evidence of the incest. I tried writing mom's friends — all denied any knowledge of incest. I doubt the incest happened so often — this impedes my recovery.

All states require professionals to report child abuse, but their training in child abuse and neglect is usually focused on patterns seen in male/female sexual abuse. The legal definition of sexual abuse requires being able to prove or disprove conclusively whether a specific proscribed action took place, or in civil cases, whether the act was damaging, and the damage can be proven.

Many cases of sexual abuse by females fit legal definitions even though the laws were typically developed to govern unwanted and/or forced adult male sexual contact with female minors. Physical evidence such as semen and pubic hairs, however, usually does not exist in sexual contact between females.

Child Protective Services workers are the frontline troops in fighting child abuse and neglect. Of the 93 mother/daughter sets in this survey, and

21

the 9 mother/son sets, none reported being investigated by a child protection agency. This result is partly a function of their ages — child protection laws, agencies and workers are relatively recent developments, especially in nonurban locales. These agencies also often operate with a bias that the child should be kept with the mother. However, the real issue is: how many sexual abuse cases are being investigated and prosecuted now?

Mothers convicted of child sexual abuse may not receive proper treatment or are treated with, or as if they were, male offenders. There may be some cases in which they are not charged with sex offenses because the social workers managing the cases know that no treatment is available even if the mother were convicted.

MENTAL HEALTH DEFINITIONS

I think therapists look for male perpetrators primarily. I think sexual abuse needs to be more clearly defined.

Mental health professionals define sexual abuse in part by its emotional effects. Therefore, they use broader and perhaps looser definitions of sexual abuse than the legal system does. These professionals must report all cases involving children or abuse of any adults unable to protect themselves. Mental health treatment of adults abused as children often focuses on the emotional effects of the abuse. However, the training of these professionals is often based on research into male perpetrators and female victims. This narrow specificity of training has been a difficulty for many of the survivors.

I would like therapists to recognize some pattern that must exist. Perhaps it is the portrayal of the client/patient's mother as angelic, perfect, nonsexual or the client's inability to discuss or tolerate discussion of anything negative about mother.

Many of the daughters are convinced there is a significant difference between sexual abuse by mothers and abuse by male offenders.

[It is] difficult to believe that it happened and is more subtle than father/daughter sexual abuse. It takes much longer for it to come to the conscious mind than abuse by a male. How much more vulnerable the client feels dealing with mother's abuse than father's abuse.

22

FINKELHOR'S STANDARDS

Dr. David Finkelhor, a noted researcher into child sexual abuse, conceived of criteria frequently used by other research professionals to define child sexual abuse (see Finkelhor, 1986, pp. 180–198). His criteria can be easily applied to many of the findings of this survey. Finkelhor's criteria for child sexual abuse include traumatic sexualization, betrayal, powerlessness, and stigma.

Traumatic Sexualization

By this, Finkelhor means "premature and inappropriate sexual learning" by the child. The child loses sexual innocence and sexuality likely becomes a source of confusion and/or emotional pain. One respondent in this study described such an experience:

[Her fondling my buttocks and upper thighs and being made to sleep with her] are all I remember — it's enough. The sexual intent was clear as was the message that I was only something to be used by someone I thought loved me. I also consider the turning us over to our uncle [who sexually abused me and my siblings] to be sexual abuse on her part. She did more than ignore it — she arranged it.

Trauma from sex is a common experience among respondents, and many have struggled for years to resolve their pain.

Betrayal

Finkelhor defines betrayal as "a violation of trust and dependency" through activities and events "which the child later comes to feel were wrong and selfish."

This is the worst kind of theft possible … theft of one's childhood, theft of hope, theft of trust, theft of reality, the loss of a parent, the loss of innocence, mostly the loss of safety.

Many of the daughters feel they were abandoned as children, not physically perhaps, but their childhood needs became secondary to their mothers' needs. Many believe their mothers were unforgivably selfish.

It's a different kind of betrayal, it confuses our sense of self, our boundaries, who we are, the parent or the child. I resented fulfilling my mother's needs, she was supposed to fulfill mine.

Powerlessness

Finkelhor proposes that a child experiences powerlessness when "coerced by force, threats or deceit to submit to boundary violations."

> My mother threatened to burn my hair/me if I did not comply. I was given beer to drink. I was beaten and there were threats that I would be burned if I wasn't quiet. Sometimes I was slightly burned on the buttocks with lit cigarettes. I learned not to cry and to stop screaming. Sometimes I remember these experiences as ones that I witnessed from across the room. Most of the time my mother did this sort of thing to me alone. Other times my father was involved as well. They also inserted objects into my vagina and/or rectum. My mother at least once made me lick her vulva and touch her anus. She showed me a lit safety match and threatened to burn the hair off my head if I didn't do it.

While not every daughter in this survey experienced the level of coercion and threat this daughter did, most felt compelled to submit to unwanted sexual experiences. For example, although the following daughter did not experience direct, physical threats, she was aware of the coercion and pressure applied to force her silence.

> When I was very young, my mother used to drive all us kids out a lonely, isolated country road. Then she'd drop some of my kittens out the door. She'd drive ahead, turn around, then drive back past the kittens crying on the road. This was called "abandoning." Later she threatened that if I told anyone about any of the abuse, by anyone, I'd be taken to an orphanage and never see my family again. I believed her. I knew how easy it was for her to abandon small, vulnerable creatures.

This daughter's mother, to this day, presents herself publicly as deeply concerned and caring about her daughter.

Stigma

Stigma occurs when "the secrecy causes the child to fear blame for the adult's actions." As little girls, these daughters were often, no matter how much or little they may have understood it, sexually active with the partner of a grown male. This fact alone may have been enough to ensure silence. As the girls grew older, they were exposed to the homophobia of our society, causing additional fear and concern.

Furthermore, for the rest of their lives, they know something about their mothers that no one else likely knows, something in stark contrast to what daughters know is socially acceptable behavior in mothers. What are they to do with such knowledge?

I felt like I had a deep, dark secret even in the survivor's group.

THE CRITICAL ELEMENTS OF SEXUAL ABUSE BY MOTHERS

Formulating definitions of sexual abuse by mothers and other females requires information from adult survivors about what was abusive, what was damaged, and what keeps this abuse hidden. The survey sought to elicit such information:

Q. What did you experience that you considered abusive? The statement of this daughter illustrates the range of elements the respondents considered abusive:

[We need to know] the different forms [of abuse by females] from overt genital contact to inappropriate relationships and touching, ritual cleaning, exhibitionism, obsession with the child's sexuality and/or health, fusion and "boundary problems," permissiveness, etc. — to help validate the survivor's experience as real and significant.

Other respondents experienced a single, but often repetitive act, which they considered abusive.

I think that most women (and men) do not understand how many different ways someone can be sexually abused. I just learned that repeated, daily enemas for 7 years was sexual abuse when a friend shared her story with me. I just didn't know THAT qualified! Please define what sexual abuse is and can be!

Elements of this abuse are tied to the uniqueness of mother/daughter relationships, including the daughter's loss of mother as the primary source of nurturing and protection.

Q. What was it that was damaged in you by the sexual abuse by your mother?

There is a different quality to being abused by a mother as opposed to being sexually abused by anyone else. This is difficult to explain. It may have to do with the devastation and betrayal of the mother-child bond.

In addition, when daughters are sexually abused by their mothers, the daughters become vulnerable to abuse and neglect by others. Only two percent (2%) of the 93 daughters reported being protected by their fathers or any other adult. The mothers may have surrounded themselves with adults whom they were sure would not question their abusive behaviors. They may have chosen adults they could dominate or who would participate in the abuse, thus insuring their silence. Whatever the cause of the non-protection by the other adults, it remains a significant element of abuse of daughters by their mothers.

> Since mothers are expected to be [the] primary caretakers physically, emotionally, etc., I feel that abuse by a mother is <u>very</u> damaging, especially if the father is absent [in <u>any</u> sense], and the family is isolated.

INTENT IN MOTHER-PERPETRATED SEXUAL ABUSE

Issues of intent often arise when examining sexual abuse by mothers because childcare often requires acts of physical intimacy with a child. However, the caretaker role often provides mother perpetrators with a protective cloak of purported maternal solicitude that shrouds abuse. About half of the daughters reported feeling sexually abused by administration of enemas. This is an example of the fine line between legitimate care and sexual abuse.

Before the advent of antibiotics, enemas were commonly used to reduce a fever. At one time, it was also considered important for a child to have a daily bowel movement, and enemas were the standard treatment for problems with elimination. In cases where enemas were used for these purposes, the mother's intent was likely the child's health, no matter how the child experienced the procedures.

What, then, do we make of stories told by daughters whose mothers gave them enemas for hours at a time? Some report their mothers breathed heavily or moved rhythmically with moans and even climactic shuddering.

Other daughters tell of mothers who seemed to re-enact near rape scenes by forcing the enema fluids into the child's body. The mothers often demanded total compliance and silence. These mothers may also have seemed aroused and perhaps orgasmic.

Sometimes these activities became ritualized and recurred over many years. This is not normal childcare, and the mothers' intentions and actions are at best questionable, at worst harmfully excessive.

Even professionals find it uncomfortable to make judgments about mothers' behaviors. Perhaps such cases will force us to re-examine child-care, mother and child relations, and female sexuality. Standards are needed with which we can make judgments about intent and effect. Some incidents seem to be in a "gray area" because the intent or cause are unknown, creating a difficult situation for the survivor to understand or resolve.

It happens even when a mother loves and treasures her child very much and doesn't want to hurt her.

No matter what the mother's intent, the impact of sexual inappropriateness needs to be revealed and validated. Most survivors want to be heard, believed and healed; they want to be able to go on.

It is still a rape of a child, meant to intimidate, humiliate and control.

APPLYING FINKELHOR'S CRITERIA

The following are descriptions of events reported by individual daughters that seem to satisfy Finkelhor's criteria (1986, pp. 180–198) as noted:

There was weird stuff about:
- me trying on bras in the store
- her hemming my clothes
- her selection of and comments on my clothes
- her giving me unwanted sexy nightgowns and robes and teddies
- her playing with my fingers and putting her arm around me in church
- her arranging my dates
- her coming around when I was working where she worked
- my telling her all the graphic details about dates
- my telling her about my crushes
- her control of my relationships with boys
- me asking permission to use birth control
- her playing with my hair
- her intense squeezing while hugging me and repeated kisses (not on the mouth).

In general please put more questions about covert, psychological abuse on the survey. My mother and I were lovers, but it wasn't in the obvious ways.

Does this kind of behavior constitute sexual abuse? Are we uncomfortable with it? Are we uncomfortable calling it sexual abuse? Lastly, do we already have adequate categories for these behaviors such as "an overbearing mother," or would we perhaps say, "She wants to be 'too close' to the daughter"?

Is there traumatic sexualization? Yes, apparent from the existence of the list and its wide range of sexualizing behaviors. Is there betrayal? Yes, there was a violation of the daughter's trust in church, in stores, in public places; there was a violation of dependency in her intrusive control of the daughter's relationships. Is there powerlessness? Yes, in the power of the purchase of sexualized sleepwear and other clothing and in the control of relationships. Is there stigma? To the extent that this daughter characterizes this list as "weird stuff" and her relationship with her mother as that of "lovers," yes, this daughter feels stigmatized.

We *must* be willing to hear the survivors' stories. The daughter quoted here reports elsewhere in the survey that between the ages of 3 and 24, her mother physically fondled her breasts, nipples, anus and other areas; gave her repeated enemas; watched while she was made to strip off her clothing and made her change into a sexy nightgown; watched her bathe and shower, masturbate and insert tampons. The daughter was also made to watch her mother dress and undress, bathe, go to the bathroom, expose herself, and to sleep with and help her mother dress. This daughter goes on to say:

> This is NOT blame-the-mother-for-everything. I do NOT identify with people who say, "Oh, I had problems with my mother, too." This is a horse of a different color and quite serious. All I have to do is say something relatively innocuous (and nonsexual) that my mother did and people blanch. Of course, no one in my childhood environment said anything. I'm not clear how much my mother passes for normal, but she's definitely not. It could be that the people who say they had problems, too, are in denial about the seriousness of their problems.

Thousands of women might read this and say their mothers did some of these things. Some may say their mothers might now ask about their bra size, and that can be viewed as just "woman talk." At what point would such a question become abusive, even to an adult woman? What if the mother were to ask about her daughter's bra size every time she sees her daughter? Once a day? Five times in one day? Fifteen? What if she didn't ask often, but always attempted to fondle the daughter's breasts while asking? What if the mother asks it only in the company of men the mother is attracted to? What if she says she thinks about her daughter's breasts often? Says she fantasizes about them? What if she asks to see them? What if she asks to suck them or actually did suck them when the daughter was twelve? What if she says she's had orgasms thinking about her daughter's breasts?

Is it sexually abusive for a mother to place a lit candle in her four-year-old daughter's vagina? To force her to lie still this way while prolonged prayers are said over her so she will be purified and redeemed of her "sins"? The child must either accept this image of herself as "bad and sinful" and her mother as such a role model or she must reject her mother and be left with perhaps no model to use while growing into a woman. The integrity of such a child's body would be violated, and she likely feels sexually confused and traumatized.

Would it be sexually abusive for a mother to give repeated enemas while telling the child these messages? Is it sexually abusive for a mother to give a child repeated enemas, never say a negative word, but to appear sexually aroused? To continue the activity until she has an orgasm?

The single answer to all of these questions has to be, "Yes."

Is semen involved in these examples? No. Pubic hairs? Highly unlikely. So how could abuse be proven in such cases without reliable, adult witnesses? I have spoken with many police officers, protective service workers, prosecutors, judges, etc., around the country who struggle with these questions.

Is our society ready to allow its abused members (in this case, women) the power to define what's abusive (i.e., define reality)? We must understand how women can be abusive in ways different from men, from male sexuality and from the social stereotypes as mothers, women, and nurturers.

LOSSES IN MOTHER-PERPETRATED ABUSE

The definition of mothers' abuse of daughters must also include the daughters' loss of childhood in the mother/child relationship. Responses to the survey revealed that many young daughters were required to focus on and meet their mothers' needs and demands. This inversion of the daughter/mother relationship often starts in early childhood and continues into adulthood. Sometimes the pressure to nurture lasts until the mother is aged or dead and often causes resentments in a daughter.

> She wants me to love her like her own mother did when she was little and sick. It makes me nauseated to think about it. She used me to maintain her own sick pleasure. I was mother, father, husband, sister, lover and friend to her when I needed a mother.

29

As a society, we assume automatically that mothers are nurturing their daughters. However, the definition for abuse by a mother must include the recognition that a sexually abusive mother is often lost to the daughter as a functioning socializer and role model. This must be understood as a fundamental element of mother/daughter sexual abuse.

Some mothers refused to give any information on sex or birth control, and survivors have told me they became pregnant as teens because of that refusal. Some mothers told their daughters terrible things about their bodies, sex, males, sin, and their futures. Several of the respondents reported their mothers refused to deal with the onset of the daughters' menses. These actions may not seem abusive at first glance, but I feel it is wrong for a sensitive eleven-year-old girl, as in one case, to have to hide the use of sanitary napkins from her mother.

A daughter does not have a functioning mother/female role model when the mother crosses the daughter's sexual boundaries. Society expects daughters to learn about parenting, femininity, personal hygiene, and sexuality from their mothers. Society will deem the daughter aberrant if she deviates from its standards of "normal femaleness." However, our society does not look closely enough at mothers for pathology or deviance, a significant omission when we consider that society is founded on the assumption that mothers will bond with daughters and raise them to be in turn competent mothers.

In-Home Orphans and Family Scapegoats

An ingredient in abuse by mothers includes lack or destruction of any bonding between mother and daughter. Sexual abuse of a female child by her mother deeply violates the child and can make the child into an "in-home orphan" or the proverbial "motherless child." They may become "emotionally stray children" in the sense that unattached animals are "strays." The problem for these girls is that they were still living in their mother's houses while the rest of the world neither saw nor understood their fundamental aloneness. Being an "in-house orphan" is at the very least lonely and painful. Some are ignored and separated from the family circle. Many feel their mothers never cared or no longer care about their daughters' well-being.

I never got to be me. Find out who, what, when, where, why I was.
She did more than sex.

She took me out of me then told me I wasn't enough. Used, abused and thrown away.

Beyond the breakdown or aborting of the mother and daughter's relationship, disruption of the child's relations to others may follow. This may be in part because some mothers send signals that the daughter is unwanted, unprotected and unvalued.

Under these circumstances, some girls become at best the family scapegoat, but for others, that may be an understatement. Many "orphans" become the recipient of family rage and aggression. At its worst, it is a very, very dangerous position for a child. Among respondent daughters, 71% were sexually victimized by other adults and children following the sexual abuse by their mothers. These "orphan" daughters may have never had a sense of being loved and protected by a parent and family. They will hear about it for the rest of their lives, but they may never have experienced it in an uncontaminated way. Their experiences may make them settle for inadequate or abusive relationships and make them vulnerable to false promises of protection.

Without the supportive protection of a parent/child relationship, it is difficult for a little girl to grow and flourish. Too much of her time is spent in self-protection and coping with wounds and losses.

Some "in-home orphans" are murdered. Others, as adults, die prematurely. Many do not understand how they remained alive or survived their childhoods.

There is probably greater potential for in-house abandonment to occur through rejection and abuse by mothers than by fathers. This does not negate the damage of sexual abuse by fathers, but we cannot ignore the potential for profound damage to an unbonded daughter who loses the protection of her mother who may be the lynch-pin of protection. In reality, many abused daughters may remain unbonded throughout their lives, and some are unable to bond with their own children.

Fusion

Another aspect of mother/daughter abuse is fusion of mother and daughter initiated and maintained by the mother.

I was not a separate person to her. In her mind we were fused.

This fusion may seem the opposite of being an in-house orphan, and in some ways, it is. There may be no violence, but the mother exerts extreme possessiveness disguised as protection. These children's growth and development are often distorted by mothers who demand their time, energy, absolute loyalty, love, focus and support, but who give little if anything in return to the child:

> [Another] thing has to do with identity. My mom's needs dominated every aspect of my life and she saw me as an extension of her. As an adult, at age 35, I am just beginning to differentiate myself and find my own likes/dislikes and talents. Because my mom told me over and over how wonderful, brilliant and talented I am, I have suffered between extreme grandiosity and feeling like sewer scum.

One way these mothers relate is to be lover-like: jealous, seductive, expecting to be treated as a mistress rather than a mother.

At another extreme, some fusion mothers are violent, controlling, and aggressive. They expect the child to respond as if the mother has the power of a slavemaster. They also may be obsessed with the child's body and treat the daughter like a possession to be kept, discarded or given away.

> We need to define sexual abuse in terms that include [elements like] obsessions with the development of the daughter's breasts, etc.

Many fusion mothers fall between these two extremes but can or did behave at times in one extreme or another. Ultimately the children of fusion mothers are not allowed to be themselves, grow freely, or develop naturally. They are made vulnerable to further abuse by not being allowed to establish normal limits with their mothers so that they can comfortably establish them with others.

> This is a very important issue to me. To quote from The Courage To Heal: "Since children frequently bond most closely with their mothers, abuse by mothers in particular, can leave a child with severe lack of boundaries between herself and her offender." (p. 97) That expresses my own experience so well.

Such fusion can be lifelong and emotionally suffocating, causing the approach or thought of the mother's death to be unnerving.

> I used to worry about this all the time and her death was extremely traumatic for me. I never made the connection — it's fusion!

These mothers also cease to be appropriate parents when they act out their needs at the expense of their children. When the fusion is overwhelming, the child may rebel and flee long before she is prepared to live outside a protective circle or without adult guidance. Some daughters explode out of childhood.

WHAT KEEPS ABUSE BY MOTHERS HIDDEN

Much of the abuse described by the survivors in this study would be defined as sexual abuse according to child abuse and neglect laws. However, many of the survivors are still reluctant to reveal their experiences. This may be true on the personal, family and social levels.

On the personal level, children only get one biological mother, and even if they can get some nurturing needs met by others, they are loathe to risk totally rupturing the mother/child relationship. Biological mothers have enormous power to validate the lovableness and value of children. This child within us as adults seems to believe that, more than any other person, Mother can convince the world that we are worthwhile human beings. Mothers can convince us of that, and we have seen the mothers of serial killers, assassins and assorted social outcasts appear on television proclaiming their accused child's innocence and value; abused children want it, too.

To relieve a mother of the power to be "My Mom" in a world of people who have moms, to stop trying to win her love, or to say her love doesn't matter, would be like using a trapeze without a net. It can be done, but it's very risky, even with good training.

At the family level, abused children know the seriousness of accusing a family member's mother, daughter, grandmother, aunt and wife of sexual abuse. We will later see that mother perpetrators may, in fact, take on one child victim rather than multiple victims, and there is often in these families many reasons for disbelief and denial. Many daughters know that if forced to choose, they will be the ones who are shunned, ostracized, excluded from the family circle. Given the 71% subsequent sexual abuse rate reported by the daughters, these are often harsh choices and lessons in their lives.

If abused children reveal the sexual abuse by their mothers too freely, they risk not being seen as victims but as so strange that even their mothers didn't love them. They risk making others uncomfortable by challenging the stereotypes and the social mantra that "mothers love their children, mothers love their children, mothers love their children." It's easier, simpler, cheaper and emotionally less taxing for society to blame the daughters.

TOWARD A SURVIVOR-CENTERED DEFINITION OF ABUSE

Society and its agencies will continue to struggle to define sexual abuse by females. Our long history of double standards in judging men's and women's sexual behaviors will continue to hinder the effort. Another factor will be society's difficulty with female sexuality. When the subject of men and sex comes up in casual conversation, it is common to hear women say, "They all want the same thing." When women and sex comes up, men are apt to say "What do women want anyway?" We have a limited social and emotional ability to perceive the range and breadth of women's sexuality. Until we can see women as fully human and fully sexual, as capable of all human behaviors, good and bad, we will have difficulty understanding female or mother sex offenders.

Sexual abuse by mothers is often concomitant with emotional and physical abuse. As a society, we do not deal well with these forms of abuse (especially in mothers), and this, too, will hinder us.

The participation of multiple perpetrators will continue to be problematic. Other perpetrators may be easier and more familiar for the rest of us to comprehend and therefore easier for victims to reveal. Thus, abuse by mothers may remain hidden longest and be more open to questions of validity than abuse by males.

CHAPTER 2

Hiding the Horror:
The Concealment of Sexual Abuse by Mothers

Sexually abusive mother/child relationships are concealed from public view. Beverly James and Maria Nasjleti (1983) have written an important statement about female sex offenders:

> Describing and categorizing the sexual victimizers of children is an attempt to clarify what our own and others' experience has taught us. We sometimes feel like the seven blind men who tried to describe different parts of an elephant. There may be a large female elephant near us; we do not see her, but we sense that she is near. (p. 21)

Sexually abusive mothers may present only public images seen as socially acceptable throughout their entire lives. Each new study of female sex offenders therefore seems to reveal only a glimpse of clandestine offenders, like the elephants James and Nasjleti describe. Logic says they must exist. Our lack of knowledge contributes to the conclusion that sexual abuse by mothers is rare, or non-existent, or that if it does occur, it is perpetrated only by extremely mentally ill mothers.

> Validation is particularly important because of societal denial of abuse by mothers.

These mothers are not acknowledged by society, and therefore, are free to abuse with almost total impunity. Like spiders in an abandoned shed, they can catch their child victims in immobilizing webs and operate without concern about public monitoring.

Their abusive webs are not entirely of their own making. They are part of an interplay of mothers (and the imagery of mothers and mothering) and society. This society wants desperately to believe that mothers are inherently good, loving and protective of their children. One strand of the web comes from an abusive mother and says, "I love my child." That strand connects perfectly to a corresponding, widely held social belief and stereotype that "Mothers love their children." Another strand of the web says, "I'd never hurt my child" and connects to, "You're never safer than in your mother's arms."

Asked if they believe society is as willing to face mother/daughter incest as other forms of incest and sexual abuse, 87% of respondents to the survey answered "no," 11% were unsure, and only 2% said "yes." Even though they are now adults, they know that many children are nearly invisible victims tied dependently and emotionally within the webs spun by abusive mothers. These respondents know that if these children reveal the abuse, they risk losing their mothers. So the respondents know well that such children exist and that they remain silent. In addition, the respondents know that, like insects caught in webs, these children are given little thought by society; however, the respondents expressed hope that the study would change that situation, as one eloquently noted:

> I work in a daycare center where child abuse is discussed frequently and even there, I hear uninformed comments about what constitutes abuse and what kind of people abuse children. I think it's important for people to realize that perfectly loving and seemingly well-adjusted mothers are capable of abusing their children. They need to know, too, that children love their mothers despite the most horrifying abuse, and it can be more damaging to confront or condemn mothers in front of the children.

The survey explored reasons for the concealment and social denial of mother/daughter sexual abuse:

	Yes	No	Unsure
Q. Do you believe mother/daughter incest is:			
Different from other forms of incest?	77%	11%	12%
More isolating than male/female incest is?	75%	5%	19%

[It may be more isolating] because of its rarity and the [limited] social response, but not inherently.

In some ways. But pain is pain, and it would be bad [to suffer] male/female [abuse] too, so I'm not totally sure.

ISOLATION

The isolation created by such abuse is experienced in several forms:

It's very lonely and very hard to heal from because it gets so ingrained in one's sense of self.

[I have] a fear or an inability to become or feel close to other women.

Isolation from Others Abused by Mothers and/or Women

We victims feel alone in our abuse and I think we need to find a way to connect with other women who have been abused by mothers.

That we "hunger" to find others like "us." It proves our existence — or validates it, gives us relief from isolation.

There is often a powerful impact on survivors when they meet others similarly abused:

I strongly recommend that women abused by their mothers get the chance to talk with other women with the same experience. It helps the SHAME. Incest survivors in general help one another a lot, but in this

> instance I find I share more openly, honestly and emotionally with women who've gone through the mother stuff.

> After meeting survivors who have had no prior contact with other survivors (of mother/daughter sexual abuse) — I am convinced of the huge importance of as much contact as possible. I feel so sane with other survivors.

Concealment

In answer to the question, "Has (the abuse by your mother) been the most hidden aspect of your life?" 81% said yes, 10% said no, and 9% were unsure.

> The secrecy was a key element of the trauma. All this stuff going on with no outward acknowledgment was terrorizing!

The concealment, like the isolation, can be both internal and external, as one added:

> [It is] mostly from myself.

The concealment of sexual abuse by mothers is due to the children's fear of exposure and rejection or that others will fail to understand. The survivors are very careful in choosing to whom they reveal the abuse. The average number of people respondents to this survey had told was 18, though this number is likely to be high because several respondents had spoken to large groups. My guess is that the number of true confidants is likely two to five people.

Revelation/Disclosure: Whom They Tell, and When

Asked to estimate the amount of time that passed between the actual abuse and their reporting of it, two percent of the survivors reported telling an adult at the time of the abuse. This percentage is low perhaps because of the socially reinforced dictum, "Little girls do not tell on their mothers." Also, there may have been few trustworthy adults to tell. Two percent told another child at the time the abuse. One percent indicated: "I told someone ___ days later." None responded: "I told someone ___ months later." Fewer than 5% told someone about the abuse within one year. More than 95% did not tell anyone during childhood.

On average, they did not tell anyone about the sexual abuse by their mothers for 28 years. There was a range of 1 to 63 years between the abuse experience(s) and revelation of it.

Never occurred to me to tell her to stop, threaten to tell, or tell someone else.

The survey responses revealed that only 5% of the daughters made efforts to tell anyone about the sexual abuse during childhood. Only 3% actually did tell someone else, while another 2% threatened to tell.

Who Knew About the Abuse?

The survey posed the following question, and the percentages of responses are as follows:

	Yes	No	Unsure
At the time I was abused by my mother:			
My "other parent" knew the abuse was happening	20%	27%	53%
Other non-parent adults knew I was being abused	28%	27%	36%

One in five respondents report that their "other parent," usually the biological father, knew of the sexual abuse by the mothers. More than half the daughters were unsure if the other parent knew about the abuse. In addition, some of the other parents contributed to denial and confusion that followed the sexual abuse.

[My father knew] and participated and probably initiated it !

My father not only condoned her [my mother's] behavior but enforced my submission to it; he hit me when I "gave her lip" [i.e., said no].

[He was in] denial but he did it, too. [He] covered up for her.

I'm adopted. In terms of the more subtle emotional stuff (I'm not sure my father knew). Not sure [who knew] about the physical stuff.

The "other parents" may not be reliable sources of information in protective services investigations. They are highly unlikely to report sexual abuse of their children by their wives to authorities. All too often, both parents are involved or gain some sort of advantage by not disclosing.

Many respondents were unsure whether other adults may have known. One quarter (25%) believe other adults knew, and one reported being told some details as an adult by a relative who knew of the abuse when it occurred.

Talking the Talk

Fortunately, 98% of these daughters report they now have someone they talk to about the abuse. Some speak to friends (88%). Friends are the overwhelming first choices as confidants about the abuse. The survivors turn to those who are close but *outside the family circle*. This communication may also be detailed, because they apparently talk about it very little outside these friendships.

But I still hold back some things.

Some spoke to siblings (7%). There is little talk about the abuse between the survivors and their siblings. This conversation may be very controlled exploration and limited to one sibling. Others speak to therapists (3%), but none reported speaking to another survivor (0%), therapy group members (0%), or self-help group members (0%).

These responses are shocking to me because 81% of these daughters report that they are *currently in therapy*. Perhaps these responses mean that their first choice is their friends, but they can also talk to their therapists. However, the picture painted by these numbers may be accurate and may account for many therapists' reports that they've never treated a case of mother/daughter abuse.

That the daughters are not talking with other survivors or in group therapy is also surprising. However, my own clients have often needed much encouragement to expand their support systems. These responses may also indicate that many may require special services and groups such as the group available to the following survivor:

[I have spoken to] selective people like my therapist. I spoke of this at SIA meetings,[1] *but really* talk *about it with others [only] at SIA/Women Abused by Women meetings.* Never to non-survivors.

None (0%) reported speaking with spouses or partners. I find it hard to imagine, and sad, that the 93 women in this survey (44% of whom are in long-term relationships) do not talk to their spouses or partners about the abuse.

In addition, none (0%) reported discussing the abuse with ministers, priests, rabbis, or other clergy. These data are sad but not surprising. Many religious institutions have been a source of messages and rules such as, "Love your mother at all costs." Why would these daughters turn to institutions that regularly promote mother/daughter banquets and Mother's Day services but may avoid acknowledging child abuse, even when it occurs among their own personnel or in their own institutions? I have met only one religious professional who acknowledged the existence of sexual abuse by mothers. It is to be hoped that religious organizations will become much more honest than they have been about the range of family experiences and can then begin to offer comfort to these daughters.

None of the respondents reported discussion of the abuse with the other parent (father). These men did not protect their young daughters, even though many knew of the abuse.

The respondents report not discussing their abuse with their own child or children (0%). During the daughters' adulthood, virtually no discussion of their childhood abuse with their own children, if they have any, occurs. The now-adult daughters' perpetrators (mothers) have become the daughters' children's grandmothers. These children may have a very different relationship with the grandmothers than the daughters had with their mothers as children. The sexual abuse experienced in childhood may also raise fears in the adult survivors about being parents. However it occurs, the intergenerational silence allows female offenders to remain hidden within their own families.

None of the respondents discussed the matter with colleagues (0%) or others (0%). We may all know a silent survivor of a mother's sexual abuse.

---

[1] Survivors of Incest Anonymous, a national 12-step self-help group modeled on the processes of Alcoholics Anonymous.

At this point, we know very little about sexual abuse by mothers and probably nearly as little about sexual abuse by females in general. We have not created a social climate in which we will be educated.

Adult Discussion of the Abuse by Mothers and Daughters

Society has a strong expectation that mothers and daughters will maintain life-long contact; most of the survivors have had adult contact with their mothers. They were asked:

	Yes	No	Unsure
Q. During your adulthood:			
Has your mother tried to talk with you about the sexual abuse?	8%	91%	1%
Have you tried to talk with her about (it)?	29%	70%	1%

The communications picture is clear. Few women talk about this abuse except the survivors, and even then seldom outside a very trusted circle of friends.

THE NEED FOR ANSWERS

Do mothers and other females sexually abuse children?

Why don't we know more about this?

How damaging is it?

How much of it is occurring?

How could we not be aware of it?

Are we ready for the truth?

In defining and reporting what is sexually abusive between females, society will have to empower females to control their own bodies and sexuality whether or not a man is involved. The power to say, "No" sexually will have to rest squarely in the hands of a victim and be enforced by law and social mores. If our society chooses to ignore reports of sexual abuse of a female by another female, we will be telling children that what happens to them doesn't matter. Women by the thousands are going to say it does matter and demand that we respond. The process of defining and learning more about sexual abuse by mothers and other women is currently occurring primarily among the survivors themselves. We will need to learn from them. They are the ones who can and will answer our questions on this issue.

CHAPTER 3

The Survey

This book reports and analyzes a survey of 93 volunteer, adult women across the nation who self-reported sexual abuse by their mothers, primarily but not exclusively during their childhoods. They provided this data in 1990, after hearing about the study in several ways: 22% at a conference or workshop, 56% through "my therapist," and 22% in other ways. There were no responses to surveys through direct mail contact.

The goal was to study the adult daughters of mother offenders, but a small study of 9 men was also conducted. The samples are of vastly different sizes, and data from the sons presented in Appendix A are considered *tentative*.

Over 500 survey items focused on five major areas:

1. **Survivors and the survivors' families of origin**

2. **The abusive experiences**

3. **Impact of the abuse on the survivors' development**

4. **Major areas of impact on the survivors**

5. **Daughters' therapy experiences**

The first four areas are presented in this volume; a second volume on treatment implications will follow.

VALIDITY OF THE DATA

These data were gathered solely as self-reports, and no attempt was made at other validation. Thus, the results rely heavily on the memory and truthfulness of each respondent. Some respondents recognized this as a possible issue and reported that they had confirmed their abuse themselves.

> My aunt [mother's sister] validated it took place and that the family was "concerned" but minded their own business.

This respondent reports her aunt confirmed that the mother began the sexual abuse when the respondent was about six months old.

There is amazing similarity in many of the stories and the patterns that emerged. I was repeatedly struck that someone in Maryland told essentially the same story as someone in Kansas who told a remarkably similar story to that of someone in Oregon. This consistency will not be as apparent to a reader as it was to me as a researcher. However, even a casual reader will see some similarities in the responses.

I am anxious to see the effect of this data on current child sexual abuse cases involving mothers. Will these patterns from the past help us to see what is being hidden today? Many of the respondents hope that will be the case.

> I would be happy to fill out anything you could send. It would be nice if anything I've been through could in any way help someone else. What can I do?

Given the respondents' ages, this data reflects abuse that occurred over approximately 30 years, 20 to 50 years *in the past*. The following excerpt from a survivor's poem expresses what it's like to look back on such events now.

> Untoward sounds
> in unwriteable sentences
> A wealth of white-hot rage
> The continuous last picture show
> of the 50's, 60's, 70's
> TIME THAT WAS MEAN.

I believe the survivors have told their truths.

My friend Connie Simmons, MSW, has been a great supporter of this research and is an excellent therapist. One night while we were preparing data for the computer, her attention was caught by a detailed mental health diagnosis of an offending mother given by a respondent daughter. Connie Simmons pondered such diagnostic detail: "How could she know all that about her mother when she was just a kid?" I looked at the code number and knew: the respondent has a doctorate in social work and teaches graduate students. I am willing to accept the diagnosis and believe that the respondent tells the truth. Connie Simmons concurred. That particular respondent did not give her name. What would be the point of lying?

I see correlations among the survey data, my personal experience and recovery, my clinical work, and reports from many other survivors. The range and content of this data appear valid because the data are consistent with other anecdotal reports I had in many conversations with survivors of sexual abuse by mothers.

Interpretations of the Data

My knowledge of subtleties and background information, as well as my experience treating women sexually abused by women and clinical observation will make the research data more usable to the reader. I'll interpret the data where it seems necessary but will label interpretations as such.

Limits of the Survey
(The "Organic Process" Syndrome)

I see several areas that remain to be investigated. I've had to accept that there is no going back to rework such a project with what I know now, except in future research. For example, I wish I'd asked about homicidal ideation and about sexual abuse by both parents, areas I did not consider in detail. I hope in the future this data will look simple and unsophisticated, even dated, and that we know more than we do now because new studies will have been done. For now, this is an attempt to validate and support the survivors and to focus attention on the issue. Clearly, additional research is warranted.

Every effort has been made to derive data from solid and honest social science research methods. Beyond that, this has been an exploratory process. The survey instrument grew out of anecdotal reports by survivors; it may have helped some of them find greater clarity, and they taught me a great deal.

Survivors' Comments

The survivors commented on nearly every aspect of sexual abuse by mothers. In this book, the survivors do much of the reporting. The survey respondents' comments are quoted verbatim in italics.

SURVEY ASSUMPTIONS

All research proceeds with assumptions, and these were mine:

1. Some mothers sexually abuse children.

This is a simple but important point because of the isolation so many survivors feel and society's resistance to negative reports about mothers.

> *The books that barely mention it make you feel like more of a freak. That somehow you can make it and survive and function and not hurt others in spite of this.*
>
> *It does happen and we are not some freak show rarity.*

It is illogical to conclude that females, half of the human race, are so different from men that none would perpetrate sexual abuse of children.

> *It's real. Mothers do abuse their daughters. Nobody could fantasize stories this horrible.*

A few women I've spoken with have resisted the idea of mother/female perpetration research because they fear such information will be used against women in general. This attitude seems akin to not charging male pedophiles because they may be Democrats, Norwegians, or movie stars. The price of silence, of avoiding this research is too high. Would we think that African-American men should never be charged with child abuse because African-Americans are oppressed? No. The price is too high.

> *Not all women are functional. Do not put us on a pedestal.*

Asked what they wanted the general public to know about such abuse, the daughters answered with almost one voice: "It happens."

> That it exists … just like other types of abuse and it is just as important to talk about as "regular"/"normal" incest! Sad commentary, heh?

2. Sexual abuse by mothers (or any female) is damaging to a child.

Even recent professional literature has denied that sexual abuse by mothers occurs or is damaging, or it has vastly minimized the effects of such abuse.[2]

> Women can be violently abusive. It is devastating to your own sense of self worth to be so violated by your mother.

Women are capable of all human behaviors. I have found the intensity of some of the daughters' abuse histories to be personally painful.

3. Research on sexual abuse by mothers requires investigation of physical, verbal, and emotional abuse as well.

4. If confidentiality were assured, the adult survivors would give full and accurate information.

It is currently safer and easier to research sexual abuse by mothers by surveying adult survivors rather than by questioning the offending mothers directly or their current child victims. The risks for children who are currently victims and dependent upon their mothers for any degree of protection and nurture are still too great.

> I feel that research on the symptoms of a child being sexually abused [by mothers] should be done so as to more readily identify children and get them away from these parents.

The survey respondents' identities will never be revealed. Only three did not give their names. However, confidentiality didn't matter to some.

> I don't care if you put up a billboard with my name on it! I have <u>nothing</u> to hide. I did <u>nothing</u> wrong and refuse to be ashamed or coerced into silence any longer. Good luck with this work!

I feel privileged that this group trusted me with such personal information. I respect their sometimes amazing degree of honesty and fairness.

5. Some adult survivors are ready to reveal their experiences, and it would not be damaging to them.

It was assumed these individuals could make appropriate decisions about self-disclosure.

> I have been silent too long.

---

[2] For example, see Mathis' (1972) comment: "That she might seduce a helpless child into sexplay is unthinkable, and even if she did so, what harm can be done without a penis?" (p. 54, quoted in Allen, 1991, p. 12).

49

There are emotional and psychological risks in revealing the details of sexual abuse experiences.

> I cried when I got to this page of questions. As a nurse I was never able to give patients back rubs without using gloves because I hated to have hand-lotion and powder on my hands. She probably forced me to do that to her when I was young.

> This is starting to make me feel sick.

Some respondents reported that the survey was helpful.

> When I got the survey from my therapist I took some time before I even began to fill in the blanks and then once I started I couldn't put it down until I got to [the pages which ask for details about what actually happened that was sexual]. I couldn't even read them. Could not read those pages. I took the survey to my next therapy session and we did those pages together. She read aloud and wrote for me and I completed them that way. She already knew all [the answers] but we did the pages together in a warm, loving way. A safe way.

The survey alleviated the isolation for some, and others reported that it helped them explore their own experience.

> I know this survey wasn't done for me personally but if nothing else it has helped me feel like there is some group in this world that I belong to and I'm not alone. That's a pretty important thing.

Another survivor shared this response:

> I am hurting so bad right now I don't know where to turn. In answering these questions I remembered additional abuse by my mother. I am feeling very isolated.

She then described her therapy and the solid support she feels she has received to resolve her conflicts. She added a typical respondent comment:

> I am really anxious to know the results of the survey and glad to have a part in it.

Several reported they kept their completed survey forms for a while before they could mail them back.

THE SURVEY INSTRUMENT

The survey was a 17-page questionnaire placed in a plain brown envelope with an addressed return envelope. The survey often took the respondents hours to complete, which may have taken some women out of the sample group. Another research method may have gathered different data. I sent out approximately 110 surveys and received 93 (84%) back, a high return.

The Sample

I sought the sample by announcing the survey at conferences where I made presentations, contacting therapists in various parts of the country and asking them to inform others, and writing to people who had contacted me as the author of *When You're Ready.*

The Data

In this volume, the raw data are presented. Comparisons of some items from the daughters' childhoods and adulthoods are made. In addition to data-gathering, this process has been a forum — a several-year dialogue between me and a large group of women. This population is a group we have not researched sufficiently. This volume may or may not begin to change that, but at the very least it gives voice to eloquent statements like the one on the following page, which reveals why we need to hear:

I want my voice back.
I have a wonderful, lovely singing
     voice
I've been paralyzed for years from
     not letting it be heard.
Always clearing my throat instead.
Like a nervous tic in my throat.
From the decades of silence.

First I will wail a storm of grieving.
And that will lift me gently to
     resonant blues.
Then playfully reaching, stretching
     my little 3 year old arms,
     embracing peaceful, loving
     music my soul has stored in safe
     keeping all these years.
The songs my mother never sang
     me
Are songs that will never be sung.

The songs that loss stirs within me
are being born now
As I mother "my child" that never
     left.

Soon I will sing to be seen
and heard
and to know I am safe.

Part Two

THE SURVIVORS
AND THEIR FAMILIES

CHAPTER 4

The Survivors

A t the time of the survey the respondents ranged in age from 23 to 66, and the average age was 37.6 years old. The ethnic composition of the sample varied greatly from the composition of the United States in general: 90% listed ethnicity as Caucasian; only 3% identified themselves as Hispanic; the remaining 7% were distributed throughout other ethnic groups. The respondents also provided information about their levels of educational achievement: 82% have more than a high school education, while a remarkable 32% had earned graduate degrees.

Occupational information was also included in the survey. Several respondents listed more than one occupation, six listed none, and four reported they are disabled. One said she is a "recovering incest/emotional abuse survivor" as an occupational identifier. An educator said she was "presently too emotionally unstable to teach." Many of the respondents are human service graduate students in fields such as social work, law, medicine. About a third are already in helping professions as physicians, therapists, and educators.

RESPONDENT PROFILES

Table 1
OCCUPATIONS*

Student	10%
Mental health	14%
Physical health	10%
Clerical	11%
Administration	10%
Education	10%
Arts	10%
Writing/publications	8%
Laborer	7%
Law	5%
Technical	4%
Sales	3%
Research	3%
Other occupations	7%

Table 2
ANNUAL INCOME

Less than $5,000	11%
$5,001 to $10,000	11%
$10,001 to 15,000	18%
Less than $15,000	**40%**
$15,000 to $20,000	10%
$20,001 to $30,000	25%
$30,001 to $45,000	13%
$15,000 – $45,000	**48%**
$45,001 to $60,000	4%
$60,001 to $75,000	0%
$75,000 and above	5%
More than $45,000	**9%**

*Total exceeds 100% because some respondents listed more than one occupation.

Table 3
RELATIONSHIPS

Single/never married	15%
Unattached by choice due to a history of difficult relationships	9%
Single by choice	2%
Unattached currently but open to a relationship	9%
Total single	**35%**
Divorced	10%
Separated	2%
Multiple and/or brief relationships	3%
Married	23%
In long-term but unmarried relationship	3%
In long-term lesbian relationship	18%

Table 4
ETHNIC BACKGROUND

Caucasian	84%
Hispanic	3%
Asian-American	3%
African American	1%
Native American	1%

Table 5
EDUCATION

None listed	12%
High school	4%
Some college or bachelor's degree	50%
Master's degree	22%
Doctorates	8%
Medical degree	2%

Information regarding financial status indicated that a large percentage reported incomes of $15,000 or below per year, a low figure in 1990, especially given this group's level of education. Eighty-eight percent (88%) of the respondents earn $45,000 dollars or less annually. Only nine of these daughters earned $45,000 or more per year. While this is a low figure considering that the respondents included twelve with doctorates, two physicians, one attorney, one certified public accountant, an owner of a real estate firm, and two full professors, it may also reflect gender economics: in the United States women earn about 76 [according to latest figures] cents for every dollar earned by a man with similar qualifications and responsibilities. However, their level of training, the work they perform, and their obvious commitment to working for the good of others are impressive.

> Because of problems of fear, low self-esteem, anxiety, authority, attention span, etc., I've had a hard time getting and keeping jobs that pay well and utilize my talents [and I feel this is] directly related to the abuse.

The daughters were asked about their current relationship status. Relationships are important to consider because many of the daughters have withdrawn from or been pushed out of their childhood families. Their subsequent relationships may be critical sources of support.

Nine percent (9%) reported they have chosen not to be currently in a relationship. Some reported that they are so emotionally injured by their mothers' abuse, that of additional abusers, or the degree and duration of abuse, that they do not want to risk intimate human contact. These may be the grown up "stray" children mentioned earlier. There are a variety of reasons for not being in a relationship, but when one's self-esteem, body image, fear of people or further pain precludes relationships, it is cause for sorrow. Please refer to Tables 1–5 for detailed respondent profiles.

In many ways, these are ordinary American women making their way through the troubles of contemporary life. At the same time, this is an extraordinary group with a remarkable will to survive and speak their piece.

CHAPTER 5

The Mother Perpetrators

Ninety-three percent (93%) of the offending mothers were the biological mothers of the women who responded to this survey. These data are disturbing given our deeply held social belief that once a woman gives birth she will go to great lengths to protect her child. As a society faced with nearly overwhelming social problems, we want desperately to believe this is true and that mothers above all others can be trusted with this nation's children.

There were a few abusive relationships with mother figures who were not the daughters' biological mothers. Two percent of the respondents reported being abused by an adoptive mother, 1% by a stepmother, 1% by a grandmother who raised the respondent, and 1% by a foster mother who raised the respondent.

THEY ALL LOOKED SO NORMAL: SOCIAL PRESENTATION BY MOTHERS

Asked if their mothers appeared normal to people outside the home, 84 (90%) of the daughters responded yes; 7 (8%) said no; and 2 (2%) did not answer. There were aspects of some mothers' behaviors or personalities that might have caused suspicions *if others had been willing to look*. The differences between the public and private behaviors of some offending mothers is striking. That people couldn't or wouldn't see through the deceptions still angers some daughters.

The children had to bear the burden of any disclosure. Many felt betrayed and believed others colluded with their mothers by turning a blind eye to the abuse. Social acceptance of these women as normal mothers was most likely the major factor in the lack of recognition of them as sex offenders.

Nearly *every* daughter believed her mother appeared normal to those outside the family at the time of the abuse. How accurate that perception is — how much of the time individual mothers appeared normal — probably varied. However, the majority may well have been able to seem caring and concerned to those who might have helped the child.

> [She looked like a] pillar of the community. I do not believe that anyone outside of our family [and I don't know about inside either] would have seen ANYTHING to provoke suspicion regarding the nature of my mother's psychopathology, attitudes or behaviors towards me. My mother was highly educated, had successfully been a professor for several years before having children, was a volunteer in various highly regarded, "do-gooder" type organizations, was a good neighbor, knew a great deal about child psychology, and was the perfect 1950's-early 1960's support person for her husband's blossoming professional career. No one would believe what she became when left alone with me. Sometimes I still don't believe it.

> I am 100% convinced that she has NO awareness of what she did to me. She may have been in some kind of altered state when she abused me.

> She had an explosive temper and often acted paranoid.

> She specialized in being the poor, hapless victim to get people to take care of her. A couple of years ago she got a 'Volunteer of the Year' award.

It happens! [The survivors] are not queer or funny. Rape by a woman is possible. Believe the child. Pay attention.

[Her appearing normal] <u>ENRAGED</u> ME!

[Outside our home she could look] angelic and perfect.

All (100%) of the daughters said their mothers were *not* mentally retarded; in this group, it was not an issue.

[Mental retardation?] Not at all. She had a graduate degree.

PERPETUATING THE PAIN: MOTHER'S SEXUAL ABUSE HISTORY

The daughters were asked questions to discover what they knew about their mothers' possible sexual abuse histories.

	Yes	No	Unsure
Q: Do you:			
Think **your mother was sexually abused?**	51%	11%	39%
By her father?	29%	17%	53%
By her mother?	20%	29%	50%
Know **your mother was sexually abused**			
By her father?	8%	71%	20%
By her mother?	1%	20%	60%
Think **she was sexually abused**			
By another man?	19%	20%	60%
By another woman?	5%	32%	61%

Half (51%) of the daughters believed their mothers had been sexually abused. This is in striking contrast to the 94% figure gathered from female offenders in a study by Ruth Mathews, Jane Kinder Matthews and Kathleen Speltz (1989). In that study, not all the women had abused their own children, but if there were any correlation between these two female offender groups, it indicates a communication gulf between the mothers and daughters in the current study. This indication reflects the previously noted absence of any communication between the mothers and daughters regarding sexual abuse.

One respondent indicated she absolutely did *not* believe her mother had been sexually abused. Another said she questioned her own belief that her mother had not been abused. Some don't care about their mothers' previous history.

[It may be] me not wanting her to have an excuse."

Don't know. Don't care.

Potential Female Offenders Against the Mother Perpetrators

Twenty percent (20%) of the respondents believe their maternal grandmothers sexually abused the daughters' mothers, but 94% say they don't know that to be true. Significantly, only one respondent knew that her mother was abused by her own mother.

I found out the evening [after] I had attended a workshop [on mother perpetrators].

It appears that sexual abuse among women, even in the same family, is either rare or a very closely guarded secret. On the other hand, these numbers may reflect an attachment by the daughters to their grandmothers and suggest that they either don't want to know about abuse occurrences or that they have had very different experiences with their grandmothers than their mothers did. It may have been intolerable to believe or know they were from a long line of female sex offenders.

Some of the mothers became perpetrators totally outside the mother/grandmother relationship.

I know she wasn't abused by her mother.

These data, along with the daughters' own silence, support my belief that no one knows the actual incidence of sexual abuse of females by other females. It is still too volatile for women to address this issue openly.

Potential Male Offenders
Against the Mother Perpetrators

About one third of the daughters think their mothers were abused by their fathers, but only 8% know that was the case. This suggests that their grandfathers were more likely to have been the offenders than the grandmothers.

These daughters provide a striking rich and detailed description of the grandfathers who were their mothers' perpetrators. This may reflect their mothers' focus on male offenders and avoidance of female offenders. Some daughters are aware of and may even identify with their mothers' abuse histories.

> He was a drunk when she was a child. I feel pretty certain [that he sexually abused her] but it's my speculation.

Some details were likely to have been provided by mothers or other family members:

> I don't think the following info excuses her but maybe it would help you to better understand her and women like her. My mother and all her brothers and sisters were molested by their father as well as beaten. Their mother was sickly and died of cancer at a fairly young age. The girls in the family were rented out on a regular basis by their father. My mother claims to have woke up one night at the age of 12 to find a strange man in her bed. She told her father and the man she would kill them both if it happened again. The abuse stopped when one of her sisters ran away because she thought she was pregnant.

> He used to chase her around the kitchen with knives in his hand threatening to kill her and to seduce her.

About one third of the daughters spontaneously reported that their own fathers had sexually abused them in addition to or in conjunction with their mothers. In light of this information, some daughters may understandably have underestimated the potential of offending grandparents in a wish to possess some "non-offending family."

Research indicates that the children of parents who have suffered through wars and other trauma may absorb their parents' pain and memories, even if the parents never speak of them. If these daughters are in denial about sexual abuse, it may be to help their mothers retain a sense of family also.

If some of the mothers became perpetrators outside the mother/grandparent relationship, and even if they were abused themselves, it does not excuse their monstrous acts.

Other Possible Offenders Against Mother Perpetrators

About one fifth (19%) of the daughters indicated they think their mothers had been sexually abused by a man other than their grandfathers. The daughters were also about four times as likely to believe men other than their grandfathers had sexually abused their mothers (19%) than to believe women other than their grandmother had abused their mothers (5%).

> Her older brother [abused her] at age 7 or so. Her music teacher at age 16.

Mothers' Relationships with Men Other than Partners

Some daughters were aware of difficulties or abnormalities in their mothers' relationships with male relatives and attitudes toward men in general. One problem reported was misguided sexual attention. In addition, some reported that their mothers appeared to dislike and/or distrust men. The daughters do not report very positive or supportive relationships with their own fathers. Their mothers' difficulties in relating to men may compound this issue for some daughters.

> She had perverted [feelings] my grandfather would have been frightened by.

> She hates men. Mom's still so screwed up she will not speak to my son nor allow him in the house. He is age 21.

Mothers' Substance Abuse Patterns

The survey presented questions about substance abuse, and a majority of the responses indicated that substance abuse was not a problem for the sexually abusive mothers of these daughters:

	Yes	No	Unsure
Q. My mother had a problem with ...			
Alcohol abuse	32%	59%	3%
Drug abuse	19%	75%	1%

Fifty-nine percent (59%) of the respondents said that their mothers did not have an alcohol abuse problem, and 75% said their mothers did not have a drug abuse problem. However, the American Psychiatric Association (APA, 1994, p. 202) reports that in a community study in 1980–1985, 13% of U.S. adults had an alcohol abuse or dependence during adulthood. The alcohol abuse rate reported in the respondents' mothers is then 2.4 times higher than the current average for American adults.

These mothers are likely among the hidden female problem drinkers whose substance abuse often goes untreated. It should be noted that the incidence of childhood sexual abuse histories among women who become adult alcoholics is very high; a similar association may hold true among the offending mothers. Some daughters did not know the extent of their mothers' drinking problems.

> Not sure. May have during the time of the worst abuse.

□

> It's probable. It seems like there would be some alcohol (a bottle of whisky) during the Christmas holidays. There was a "joke" in my family that she would "fall up the basement steps" while doing the laundry. Looking back it seems like that was almost always during the winters when that happened — after the holidays. I certainly remember times during my childhood when there was too much drinking in our house involving both my parents. As [an] adult I could not tolerate being around them if and when they drank.

Some mothers' alcohol problems developed later in life.

> I think she does now.

Other mothers' chemical dependencies were abundantly clear.

> [She's an] alcoholic.

□

> DECEASED. From alcoholism. Cirrhosis.

Mothers' Drug Abuse

Some daughters (19%) report drug abuse among their mothers. Some mothers may have been among the women of the 1950s and 1960s who were over-tranquilized by physicians before addictions were widely understood.

She was on downers from time to time.

☐

None known, but I wouldn't be surprised. She is a sugar addict.

MOTHER AND CHILD: RELATIONSHIP DYNAMICS

Before reporting on survey responses about other family members and family dynamics, it must be noted that most aspects of the relationships between the offending mothers and their daughters were greatly troubled. On average, the abuse began when the daughters were three years old. In many cases, the mother/daughter relationship — the safe, nurturing type that society wants to believe exists — was devastated. The mothers interjected their own needs into the relationships with their daughters, causing their roles, focus and functions to become deeply disturbed. Often, the resulting problems were never resolved or corrected.

Who Is the Mother: Problems with Mothers' Role Functions

The daughters often report deep ambivalence about the women they call their "mothers." Many feel even as children they had to "mother" their mothers. Many of the survivors feel their mothers put themselves and their needs ahead of the daughters even when the daughters were very young. Such behavior was likely an attempt by many mothers to satisfy their own unmet dependency needs.

	Yes	No	Unsure
Were there problems with who was the mother and who was the child?	83%	9%	7%
Are there still problems with who is the mother?	57%	29%	12%

I have different issues [than other incest survivors]. She was my mother. The person that I spent the majority of my time with. The things she taught me are the things that I carried into adulthood. This is how you're mothered. In many ways I became her parent. I worried at 8 years old about the rent or the overflowed toilet. [Or] my brother if he didn't come home.

I was so conditioned to take care of my mother and to think of her needs that it was an earthshaking, long term shift to get it that:

1. my needs as a child were O.K.
2. she was supposed to take care of me
3. she was responsible to meet her sexual and emotional needs with other consenting adults.

Although the data indicate some of the mothers may have become healthier over time, some daughters may have become stronger at setting boundaries, or they distanced themselves from their needy mothers. Ironically, many of the abused daughters have become their aging mothers' caretakers. The daughters were asked whether problems with role definitions remain unresolved.

Yes, yes, a thousand times yes!!

YES! YES! YES!

I am the mother — she the child.

My mother is now very ill and there are times when I must be [the mother].

Many of the respondents struggle against the socially reinforced belief that adult children, especially daughters, should put a parent's needs ahead of their own. Some daughters feel guilty if they refuse to focus on their mothers' chronically needy emotional states.

> But I'm trying to learn that it's okay to be selfish so to speak and take care of me.

Prior Healthy Relationships Between Mothers and Daughters

The daughters were asked if there were times when the relationships with their mothers were healthy and functioned well. Twenty-seven percent (27%) said yes, 44% said no, and 29% were unsure. For nearly half, any positive parent/child interactions were fleeting experiences.

> Basically [it was not healthy] although there were times when we did do things like plant flowers and we would be OK just for then.

The pervasiveness of this parenting void cannot be overstated for some daughters. Memories of being nurtured and cared for by their mothers, no matter how brief or simple, may be deeply precious. Memories of being touched with kindness, of feeling accepted, understood, or valued may be tucked away and treasured like jewels. Such unmet needs in the daughters may be unsettling. Years later, as grown women, they may feel ashamed of these powerful unmet needs and their awareness of what they felt like in childhood. If the unmet needs make them similar to their mothers, they may feel even deeper shame.

Gaining Understanding: Survivors' Current Views About Mother-Child Relationships

The daughters report that they now understand that they were emotionally and/or physically tied to people who were not functioning appropriately. There isn't much comfort in it, but 92% say they understand it. Most know at least in the adult parts of their personas that there was clearly something terribly wrong with their mothers. Some can give accurate, detailed, and insightful (even professional) diagnoses of the dysfunction. At other times, however, some of these adult women mourn and ask questions such as: *"Why didn't my mother love me?" "What was wrong?" "Why did she do that?"*

CHAPTER 6

The Survivors' Families

When mothers are dysfunctional, children often demonstrate incredible resilience by turning to other members of their families for nurturance, protection, and role modeling. Children who receive such support from another family member are lucky, and, as the data in this study indicate, rare. The study asked the daughters to describe relationships with other members of their families.

OTHERS IN THE HOME: FATHERS AND OTHER PARENT FIGURES

The daughters were asked questions to determine who, if anyone, played the role of "other parent" to them during childhood. They reported the following:

Biological father	79%	Grandmother	2%
Adoptive father	3%	Stepfather	1%
Grandfather	2%		

In most cases, their biological fathers were in their lives during the actual period of sexual abuse by their mothers. This is important to consider regarding both the mothers' motivations for sexual abuse and the fathers' lack of protection of the daughters.

THE ABSENT FATHER

Uninvolved and/or "Non-Parenting" Fathers

Many of the daughters (62%) reported that their "other parents" were hardly ever around or were almost "non-persons" in the home; 32% did not report lack of involvement, and 1% were unsure. In these families with mothers who sexually abused their daughters, there is a pattern of "weak fathers" or "emotionally absent fathers." This is in contrast to the families with mothers whom the daughters frequently saw and experienced as powerful, dominating forces.

I had a father but he didn't exactly play the role of a father.

My father "reads" like the description of the mother in families in which there is father and daughter incest. He was absent from our home a lot. He typically left the house at 7 AM and returned home any time between 7 PM and midnight. He was preoccupied with professional concerns. At some point (I don't know when) he began abusing alcohol and prescription drugs, and then — maybe — other substances. He suffered(s) from severe, chronic depression and various somatic illnesses. However, the public's view of him was that he was highly successful, articulate, affable, bright, ethical, a concerned citizen, handsome, etc. At home he was mostly asleep! But he was mostly friendly in a kind of distant way when he wasn't asleep.

All he wanted was peace in his home, an absence of conflict. I became his confidant when I was about 12 or 13, listening to him describe his depression and his suicidal ideation. He was hospitalized for 14 months continuously for his depression and drug abuse (?) when I was 14 or 15. I didn't see him during that time. I don't think the hospitalization changed much.

Physically Absent Fathers

While no specific questions were asked, some respondents reported having fathers who were literally absent at times. Their physical absence may have played a crucial part in some abuse.

> My biological father, grandmother and an uncle were there sometimes and in and out of my life.

> [My father was] not home during one five year period when the abuse was particularly overt.

> Dad and Mom were divorced while the incest occurred.

> No one at home. My mother's husband, not my biological father, [was] usually 3,000 miles away.

> My father died when I was 8 years old leaving me alone in the house with my mother.

Fathers Who Were Never Present

About 10% of the daughters reported that their biological fathers were never in their lives. However, the absence of fathers as mothers' potential sex partners does not fully explain perpetration of sexual abuse. These family dynamics need further investigation with a fresh perspective regarding women's sexuality.

> [There was] no "other" [parent]. My father and mother were not married and [had] separated. I had very little contact with him. He was never around.

> No other parent figure.

Impact of Lack of Second-Parent Protection or Support

None of the daughters gave any indication that their fathers were an emotional or protective counterbalance to the abusiveness of their mothers.

This situation has also been reported in most of my contact with clients and other survivors. Our society is making a grievous error in assuming that fathers will protect their daughters from sexually abusive mothers.

When fathers are perpetrators, and mothers do not protect their daughters, we tend to see the mothers as weak, overwhelmed, trapped or afraid. We understand when the daughter victims are angry at their non-protective mothers. In cases of daughters with mothers who sexually abuse them frequently and fathers who fail to intervene, the daughters have similar feelings towards their fathers.

The picture emerges that these fathers simply did not protect their daughters. They did not intervene. There may be a variety of reasons, but the impact of their non-support is likely the same. Some fathers may have been blocked by unresolved childhood abuse experiences of their own: as one respondent noted, *"I've found out my father is a survivor, too!"*

Some of the respondents' fathers were perhaps emotionally dominated by their wives. This dynamic, however, does not fit neatly into our stereotyped views of appropriate, conventional male and female behaviors. We recognize that some men seek female partners whom they can dominate. Is there a corresponding pattern of women who look for men who previously learned to tolerate or prefer being dominated by women? Is the weakness of some fathers traceable to earlier domination by women? More research is needed.

An entangled dependency in some of these fathers, commonly seen in family members with substance abuse problems, may be occurring. Two respondents indicated such a situation:

Co-dependence.

Enabler, co-dependent and incest perpetrator.

Undoubtedly for some of the least effective fathers, the abuse of their children served to keep their wives' attention and rage focused on others. Some could not cope well with verbal and/or emotional attacks.

He'd leave when she became agitated. He left me to receive her rage and aggression. He was a first class, chicken shit coward. If he ever pushed back at her it was to save his own ass.

Inadequate personality.

NO ONE TO WATCH OVER HER: FATHERS WHO CONTRIBUTED TO THE ABUSE

At the other extreme were some fathers who brought as much or more abuse into the home as the mothers. As reported by the daughters, some of these fathers simply did not value their girl children as human beings. Some daughters became vulnerable because their mothers did not object to their husbands' aggressiveness towards their daughters or saw abuse by males as normal and acceptable behavior.

> He is a rage-aholic, obsessed with guns, withdrawn, authoritative, and abusive.

> My father also abused me physically, emotionally and sexually.

The pattern of a perpetrator-mother paired with a weak, absent, or additionally abusive and/or non-supportive father emerges frequently in this study, in my clinical work, and in informal contact with survivors. It appears to be the case in as many as 50% or more of the families reported in this study. Many of the fathers were and/or continue to be little more than sperm donors.

Other Parent's Mental Health

Nearly one quarter of the daughters indicated their fathers may have been mentally ill. The problems reported are those more expected in males than females. Some fathers came from and exhibited the typical behaviors associated with dysfunctional childhood homes. The fathers apparently received little treatment for mental health problems, as was true for the mothers. There seems to be slightly more mental impairment among the "other parents" than among the mothers.

	Yes	No	Unsure/ No Answer
Did "other parent" have a mental illness?	23%	69%	2%
Was "other parent" mentally retarded?	2%	90%	8%

I'm not sure but I think so.

◻

[My father was a] Korean War vet [and was] in and out of VA hospitals a lot. A very nervous person.

◻

My adoptive father was not diagnosed but was sociopathic.

◻

My father was an adult child of an alcoholic. [He was not mentally ill] but he battered me, too.

◻

[My other parent was my grandfather who raised me]. Maybe he was a little [retarded]. He had a good job as an architectural draftsman and just came home after work — was <u>quiet.</u> He could pretty much look normal to others but he was sort of quiet and withdrawn.

Other Parents' Alcohol and /or Drug Abuse

When asked about substance abuse by other parent figures, the responses were as follows:

	Yes	No	Unsure
Did "other parent" have an alcohol problem?	49%	46%	1%
Did "other parent" have a drug abuse problem?	5%	90%	1%

Half the "other parents" had alcohol problems, a higher rate than for American adults in general (with 13% reported by the APA, 1994, p. 202, as meeting *DSM-III* criteria for Alcohol Dependence or Alcohol Abuse at some time in their lives; *DSM-III-R,* APA, 1987, p. 173, also reports that 7% of American males are considered heavy drinkers). The relatively high rate of alcohol problems may also play a part in some sexual dysfunction in the fathers and contribute to the general sexual dysfunction in the family.

> But I don't know when these [problems] began — before, during or after the period of my abuse.

A 5% rate of drug abuse is somewhat lower than the current rate among American adults as reported by the APA (9.875%, averaging use rates from a 1991 community survey for various drugs; 1994, pp. 210, 219–220, 228, 235, 254, 260, 268) and may reflect patterns of earlier time periods.

Table 6
SUBSTANCE ABUSE BY PARENTS

Mother's alcohol problem	32%
Other parent's alcohol problem	49%
Mother's drug problem	19%
Other parent's drug problem	5%

Parents' Substance Abuse

The daughters reported on their knowledge of substance abuse by their parents (see Table 6 for a comparison of mothers and other parents alcohol and drug use). The "other parents" were primarily the biological fathers of the respondent daughters, and these men had alcohol problems at about four times the national adult average. Their rate of drug problems was significantly lower than the offending mothers' incidence of drug problems.

They Looked Normal Too:
Social Presentation by Fathers

When asked, "Could the 'other parent' look normal outside the home?" 90% said yes, 1% said no, and 9% did not respond. A few gave additional information:

Always.

My father is a federal judge.

Even though many of the fathers had serious problems, they were not obvious enough to cause forces outside the families to intervene on the daughters' behalf. With so many aggressive men in our society, little attention is paid to quiet and/or non-aggressive men whose problems are within tolerable social limits or hidden in their homes.

With 90% of both the mothers and fathers in these abusive homes capable of appearing "normal," there seem to be few cracks in these families' secretive and self-protective armor. The majority of their dysfunctions probably went undetected by those outside the home. Eighty-three percent of the "other parents" were exactly whom our society would expect them to be in traditional nuclear families: the biological fathers. These men were supposedly in relationships with the mothers, but the quality of those alliances may have been poor. Few stepfathers were reported in the respondents' families.

A few daughters report having responsible, caring grandparents:

[My grandparents] saved my life. My grandfather was my "daddy." He <u>was</u> loving but couldn't communicate well, [but he] was still capable of <u>showing</u> much emotional warmth and love. He loved me very much — they were both loving, maternal people.

Significantly, this respondent is the only one of the 93 daughters who indicated clearly that there was someone during her childhood who loved her. Her grandfather was also the only male mentioned as actively supportive of a sexually abused daughter. Other respondents reported having had grandparents who were sexual abuse perpetrators or even co-perpetrators with their mothers.

None of the respondents reported having mothers' boyfriends, mothers' female lovers, uncles, or older brothers "who was like a father" who acted as their "other parents." Eight percent (8%) indicated that some "other" person was like a parent to them but did not identify that person specifically. Some respondents identified a variety of others adults who provided parenting.

My mother's female lover lived next door.

My mother's aunt was my "other parent."

An uncle and aunt were somewhat supportive.

FAMILY BACKGROUNDS

Nearly all the abuse reported in this study took place in intact families. This fact is an important aspect of this abuse as such families are often less frequently monitored by social service agencies or others. The responses to the survey indicate that 80% or more of these abused daughters lived in two-parent homes.

> The public needs to shed the denial of incest by mothers. It does happen and we need to talk about it. Our family is full of people abused by women and men.

> It is so important that mother/daughter abuse be accepted as something that does occur in "normal families" and is not a figment of fevered imaginations.

Deeper Into the Past:
Family Histories

The survey responses are consistent with my clinical experience in that some daughters may lack information about their families' histories, especially their mothers' backgrounds. Some mothers refused to acknowledge missing siblings listed in birth records or to reveal biological fathers' identities, grandparents' names or former marriages. The daughters may discover that their families lied to them. There can be great power in such distortion and/or withholding when the mother is the major source of such information, the primary socializer, and a sexual abuse perpetrator.

Social Class

The survey included the following question:

Q. At the time of the abuse by my mother I would say my family was:

Middle class	39%
Working class	34%
Poor	15%
Upper class	10%

Most Americans seem to believe they are middle class regardless of income, and these data may reflect this bias. What is important in these data is that it's clear sexual abuse by mothers is not a lower-class, poverty-based problem. The daughters come from all social classes.

> The abuse has gone on my whole life. When it started we were poor. Now she's rich!

> [I grew up] upper middle class — professional father [and] housewife mother — both highly educated.

CHAOS AND CONFUSION: FAMILY DYNAMICS

These abusive families were often chaotic and confusing for the daughters. The abuse was so pervasive and ongoing for some that it became the reality of their early family lives.

> I was continuously moved between grandparents and parents.

> The abuse was more than a series of events; it was a context.

> As is said about alcoholic dysfunctional homes, the dramatic crisis gets our attention, but the real damage is probably done by what "didn't" happen rather than what did. I think the same thing is true for incest with regard to developing healthy self-esteem, trust, sexual identity and sexuality.

A few daughters lived in homes so sexually charged that there was no way to escape the abuse or the incessant focus on sex. In some, the sexual focus and behaviors were subtle and may have been difficult to comprehend and describe as abuse.

> The covert incest [was] — like [an] environment thick, saturated with sex — like rooms where you cannot enter without being psychologically assaulted with sex: sex crime magazines everywhere, seductive talk, ridiculing verbal molestation, extremely intrusive sex/fantasy talk, etc. And medically invasive and unnecessary procedures.

> I didn't define my abuse as sexual abuse until I was 38 years old. I was an only child. My father died when I was 8 years old and although I knew things felt wrong in my house to a large extent the physical things that went on were just the way things were.

The isolation of the abuse and lack of clarity about what was "normal" often made it difficult to know what was abusive.

> It was all tied up in basic nurturing. It was all very confusing. It was the only way to get touched, to get attention. About a year ago I was at my mother's house. We were standing out by the pool and I had a swimming suit on. She stood there touching me, first my wrist, and then sneaky feels of my breasts and my buttocks. My younger brother watched and talked with us. He didn't even notice what she was doing. She's been doing that all our lives. We were so unconscious, myself included. I was 33 years old here [at the time].
>
> A few weeks ago I told my therapist about this. She asked what would happen if I told mother to stop. I said she'd get angry. What else? She'd say I have a dirty mind. What else? I don't know.
>
> She'd stop. And she'd disassociate (withdraw) from me. As much as I hate my mother, as much as I know she'll never love, protect and care for me, and she'll never admit or apologize — a little part of me misses my mommy, and wishes she'd be what she isn't — and can't be.
>
> DAMN HER!!

Many of these families can be labeled dysfunctional to some degree by almost anyone's standards, especially when today's child abuse and neglect standards are applied. Some of the families were beyond disorganized and dysfunctional; they were pathological.

A few respondents clearly believed their families were dangerous and threatening, and they were. The following daughter notes how potentially and ultimately hazardous her mother/family life may have been.

> I strongly suspect that I had a sibling who was drowned by either my mother or one of her relatives. I only heard her talk about it once and it scared me beyond description. I believe I'm lucky to be alive.

> Without therapy and AA and friends from AA, Al-anon, COA I would be dead. The script in my family is for me to sacrifice my self in loyalty to them. I had to get off all mood-altering substances to deal with this.

Fortunately, some daughters received support from other adults. The next statement is from the oldest respondent in the survey.

> My paternal grandparents, I believe, had much to do with saving us. They lived next door and they were forever kind and loving to us, they helped us set goals as children. Although I still feel some anger I feel my life had some good direction. My therapist has indicated surprise at my wholeness regarding attitudes towards family and society. I have a younger brother I tried to protect from our mother. He now has a wonderful family, very loving and whole.

FAMILIES: OLD AND NEW

These daughters' perpetrators become their children's grandmothers. The now-adult daughters may be terrified of what the grandmother might do to their children, yet they may not have broken the silence about their own abuse. Some survivors of mother-perpetrated sexual abuse, including some respondents in this sample, may have repressed their own abuse memories and find themselves (before remembering in therapy) very uncomfortable about their mothers and children without knowing why.

Some mother perpetrators go on to offend as grandmothers, but not all do. They may be viewed and experienced by their grandchildren as much more positive maternal figures than the adult daughters have ever experienced them to be. This transformation may be a relief for the now-grown daughters, but it can also be painful. Their children may get from their grandmothers the nurture and safety that the daughters never received. The grandchildren may trust and love their grandmothers, even though the daughters may never be able to trust them, accept positive information about them as grandmothers, or love them. There may be unavoidable resentments and jealousies. Protectiveness and worry may never cease, and grandchildren's actual safety with their grandmothers may be salt in the abused daughters' wounds.

Our mythology about grandmothers is also powerful; grandmothers can be very important for grandchildren, especially in adolescence. However, we have few guidelines on how to allow our children to have safe relationships with aging parents who have histories of inappropriate boundaries with children in the past. It takes strength and clarity to draw a line, saying for example, that an aunt can change a new baby's diaper, but the child's grandmother cannot. Establishing such boundaries while maintaining contact is often emotionally messy. To withdraw often creates losses, mysteries, or disillusionment for the survivors' children.

The daughters' family lives often involve lifelong struggle. Exposure to healthier families can often be helpful and healing, but if problems arise between a now-adult daughter and her own family, she may become deeply distraught and feel like a failure.

Many survivors come to feel that by creating second, chosen families, they would finally resolve the pain of their childhood abuse, as indicated by this daughter.

Table 7
SIBLING GROUPS

	One	Two	Three	Four	Five	Six
Sisters	37%	12%	12%	1%	1%	2%
Brothers	37%	20%	7%	3%	1%	1%

[I] fantasied that they were not my real parents and that my grandmother was my mother. I fantasied that getting married would make me normal.

Some daughters of abusing mothers succeeded and now have happy family lives. However, any overlap of their families of origin and their new families can cause stress.

THE OTHER CHILDREN AT HOME: SIBLING GROUPS

Among the respondent daughters, 18% said they were an only child, 4% were adopted, and 5% were foster children. The rest had at least one brother or sister, averaging out at just under 2 each (average number of sisters was 1.8; average number of brothers was 1.7; see Table 7).

The majority of these respondents came from what are considered normal-sized American families. Several daughters had supportive older sisters who became quasi-parental figures.

My sister three years older than me played the role of the other parent. I feel like she raised me. My sister was just a kid when it started, too. She's had a lot of problems later, like me.

My older sister helped mother me when my mother was gonzo.

NOT ALONE:
MOTHERS' ABUSE OF OTHER CHILDREN

While it may be difficult for the daughters to know whether their mothers sexually abused other children or their siblings, respondents indicated that it did occur. When asked if their mothers sexually abused "other children in the family," 43% of the daughters said yes, 32% said no, and 10% were unsure. Some daughters noted details:

Cousins.

I know my mother sexually abused one older brother, suspect she did so to my other older brother and older sister. All three of them abused me [sexually and physically] so I'm interested in learning more of the generational nature of [this form of] incest.

I am a twin — the oldest by 20 minutes. While I believe my sister was not sexually abused she was emotionally abused and a witness to my abuse because we shared a room. She was a victim of our mother's 'crazy' behaviors.

The respondents were asked if they believe at least one of their siblings was sexually abused by their mothers:

	Yes	No	Unsure
Sisters	26%	44%	4%
Brothers	37%	33%	7%

Witnessing sex between my mother and sister was a key ingredient in the trauma. [When I masturbated] they secretly watched together and laughed.

The daughters often have more questions about a brother's sexual abuse than their sisters' experiences. Mother/son abuse is also a deeply hidden secret in families.

I wonder about my brother who says he is gay and slept with Mother until about age 12.

Not sure. He says no — I wonder.

Some respondents may never know if their mothers abused their brothers, but others do know:

When I told my brother I had been abused his only comment was "I'm not surprised." My brother is/was her substitute lover.

Problems Between Siblings Caused by Abuse

Many of the daughters (64%) believe the abuse caused problems among the siblings. Some believed they were the only ones in the sibling group abused by the mother, a situation that can create a deep sense of isolation. Attempts to address the abuse are often met with hostility and denial by other siblings. In addition, members of the same sibling group can have very different experiences with a parent during the same time period and in the same home.

Any remaining hostility in the daughters toward their siblings may be because abuse is often directed downward in families and groups toward targets successively less powerful. It may be dangerous to send anger up toward one's perpetrator, so it may be directed laterally, or towards younger or less favored siblings.

[It] sexualized our relationships. [We] all had to participate. They thought I was the favorite.

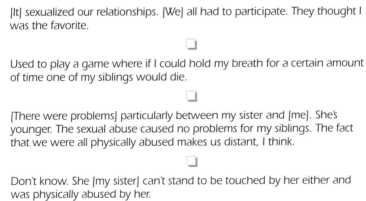

Used to play a game where if I could hold my breath for a certain amount of time one of my siblings would die.

[There were problems] particularly between my sister and [me]. She's younger. The sexual abuse caused no problems for my siblings. The fact that we were all physically abused makes us distant, I think.

Don't know. She [my sister] can't stand to be touched by her either and was physically abused by her.

Fathers' and/or Other Males' Abuse of Siblings

One third (34%) of the daughters believe at least one of their brothers or sisters was sexually abused by their fathers or other male adults who had access to them as children. Forty-three percent (43%) did not believe so, and 7% responded that they were unsure.

> My mother made my sister, age 13, sleep in the same room as my uncle (her brother) knowing he was a child molester. She admitted years later that she knew. She thought it was up to us to deal with it. If we couldn't — we were "weak." She also left all three of us alone with him and he molested all of us. When I was 16 she began to invite him for "visits" — it was my turn to be turned over to him. My stepfather "intervened" and prevented it, much to her fury — much to my relief.

This intervention is the only incident reported in the survey responses in which a father figure made efforts to protect a daughter. Clearly, these daughters were at considerable risk and, in most cases, isolated, unsupported and unprotected. There was severe disruption of the family experience for many of their siblings as well. Because the other family members are often willing to deny or collude, perhaps in self-protection, there is considerable disruption of all family relationships for some daughters. As adults, only 7% of the daughters report talking to a sibling about childhood sexual abuse by their mothers.

Part Three

UNSPEAKABLE ACTS: THE NATURE OF THE ABUSE

CHAPTER 7

Speaking About the Unspeakable:

Abuse Experiences

One of the strongest messages that was delivered through the survey responses was how important these daughters felt it was to say what they lived through — to name for themselves, for us as researchers and clinicians, and for the public what they experienced as abuse.

> It is important to share the graphic details of what made us feel molested/ abused because many things I've experienced and have heard from other women are not usually on an ordinary intake sheet at Children's Protective Services or a counseling center. Sometimes it's an attitude — the abnormally dependent, clinging attitude ... or the intrusiveness into everything private ...

"WAS IT REALLY ABUSE?": THE DAUGHTERS' EXPERIENCE

The survey posed a series of questions to gather specific data about occurrences that the daughters believe or experienced to be sexually abusive. This is important in overcoming the limits to imagining what one female could do that would be sexually abusive of another female.

Physical Fondling

Several respondents wrote about their experiences with inappropriate physical contact. During normal child care, a mother may innocently touch almost every area of a child's body. What the daughters reported is not normal child care. These daughters were asked to report *fondling* and physical contact that they experienced as sexually abusive. For example, most nonabused children *would not* report the following experiences.

Spankings sometimes gave me orgasms.

Physical stimulation of my genitals, breasts and nipples. Not fondling. Aggressive stimulation.

My mother slept with me and fondled and caressed me. [Confirmed by a relative.]

Such fondling ranged from unwanted hugging to putting "her hands all over me." Some fondling was done in ways to make it appear accidental or as part of child care. Other fondling was clearly premeditated and aggressive. The daughters' reactions ranged from physical and emotional pain to pleasure. Body areas fondled included the genitals (69% of the respondents), anus (40%), breasts/nipples (39%), inside rectum (28%), lips (16%), mouth (15%).

Most children's genitals are touched by their mothers as a part of hygiene. However, what these daughters report is different. We should accept that they know the difference between being touched and being fondled.

My older sister "diddled" me. She physically stimulated my clitoris a lot by pulling on it. I have one memory of my mother doing that.

[Fingers in] my rectum while callously putting in suppositories with sharp fingernails.

Thirty percent (30%) of the respondents report inappropriate touching of other body area(s):

She would back me up against the oven and pick my zits all the time.

[She put her fingers in my] armpits, to see if I was growing hair, [also] stroking my hair.

Since many mothers have touched their children in these body areas for legitimate reasons, what marks these experiences as sexual abuse for these daughters?

Pinching my genitals, breasts and nipples. She would masturbate by rubbing herself on me.

Oral Stimulation

The daughters reported oral stimulation by their mothers of their genitals (25%), mouth (15%), lips (17%), anus (4%), rectum (5%), and urethra (8%), while 11% reported oral stimulation in "other" locations. The oral stimulation by the mothers ranged from "kissing me all over my body," to "biting my genitals."

When I got to [this] section on oral abuse I said to myself, 'This doesn't apply to me," and I rushed right past it. My mother orally abused me. When I was a baby she would lift me out of the bathtub and hold me above her head and put her lips on my genitals. She also kissed me passionately all over my torso and lower body. I also have a memory of lying down and having her head and lips in my genitals. I think I blocked this because it's the only real physical memory I have of her doing something to me.

In my clinical practice I have observed that conscious awareness of mothers' oral stimulation of the genitals, especially to the point of orgasm, seems to be a high-voltage topic that is almost psychologically indigestible for many daughters. Addressing it is often accompanied by physical reactions ranging from gagging, nausea and vomiting to sweating, rashes, shaking and trembling or becoming "frozen."

Putting Fingers Inside the Body

Children tend to know their mothers' hands and touch better than those of any other person. A mother's hands are her body parts they experience most often. To experience her hands as both comforting and painful is confusing. For some daughters, her hands are like monsters that come in the night or into the bathtub. They report painful experiences with mothers' hands and fingers inside their vaginas (46%), vulvas (34%), rectum (34%), mouth (13%), and urethra (9%). Another 9% said their mothers had put their hands in "other" locations.

> She would "examine" my genitals sometimes.

Some daughters also reported "exams for worms," sometimes conducted well into adolescence. Some of these activities may have been legitimate child care experienced as sexual and/or abusive by the daughter. However, some had clear sexual motivations by the mothers. Some daughters reported their mothers conducted vaginal "exams" as a regular part of the daughters' teenage dating.

Putting Objects Inside the Body

One striking difference between the sexual abuse of the sons and daughters is how clearly little girls' bodies present many anatomical focal points and openings for invasive mothers. Respondents reported objects being inserted into their rectums (51%), vaginas (38%), mouth (14%), and urethra (7%). Another 7% reported the intrusion of objects into "other" locations on their bodies.

The daughters reported several types of objects often used by their mothers, including enema equipment (45%), sticks (10%), candles (5%), and vibrators (4%). Over a third of the respondents reported that "other" objects were used.

> I had no hymen and assume it was lost via a rectal tube.

Enemas were used in a medical way during many of these respondents' childhoods and these survivors often know that. For example, enemas were used to help control fevers before antibiotics were available. However, many of these reports are very sexual and non-medicinal. This is also true of rectal thermometers and suppositories.

Ah, yes, the old enema bag.

She used suppositories that she moved in and out of me until they "worked."

[She used the] black tip off the enema tube when it was disconnected.

I know she gave me enemas. I remember the can and hose. I can't remember the experience.

Judging from the written comments of the respondents, some mothers used the enemas and suppositories in very sexual and dominating ways. For some mothers, the enemas may have been a re-enactment of their own sexual abuse or rape experiences. However, this time the mother has the power and control instead of being dominated and victimized herself. The enemas often included dominance, control, rectal and vaginal insertion and penetration, injection of fluids into the child's body, and a demand for specific physical responses and surrender of something by the victim.

The respondents reported use of a wide range of additional objects, including "normal" objects used aberrantly, such as pencils, keys, hair brushes and hairbrush handles, darning eggs, light bulbs, soapy wash cloths, wooden spoons, and various fruits and vegetables. They also recount the use of clearly sexual objects such as dildos and vibrators. Daughters reported that mothers used aggressive and violent objects, including knives, scissors, lit cigarettes, sock darning tools, and surgical knives. These objects sometimes actually pierced flesh.

[She used] scissors, pinking shears, knives, and hair rollers.

[She] inserted needles into my vulva.

Some mothers used objects unknown to the survivor:

Not clear — something cold and metal

Something — I don't know what

A bottle of something cold and gooey.

Some respondents listed insertion of stranger objects, including religious medals, vacuum cleaner parts, and goldfish.

A metal garden hose nozzle and she would urinate in my face.

Surgical swabs and perhaps other medical instruments — forceps.

Some of these objects were sexual, some were perhaps fantasy objects, and some may have had significance only within the framework of a mother's mental illness.

Mothers Watching Daughters

Some of the behaviors reported by daughters as abusive may have been part of normal child care until the child was old enough to desire privacy; at that point the behaviors become invasive. In many families, the members may be comfortable seeing each other dress or bathe and not necessarily experience it as abusive. However, for these daughters, the reported watching and observing was abusive. These mothers were often very invasive of their daughters' personal boundaries and space as they bathed or showered (58%), dressed or undressed (52%), defecated (38%), urinated (34%), or masturbated (18%). Another 12% of respondents reported their mothers' intrusion during "other" activities.

She made me strip in front of her and change into a sexy night gown. She also watched while I inserted tampons.

When I was an adolescent and the abuse had stopped she would wait until I was in the bath tub and come in and go to the bathroom and stay until I got out of the tub. She would watch me defecate if she got the chance.

She watched while I masturbated but I didn't know she was there. She used to punish me for touching myself.

Bursting into the bathroom to find out what I was doing. Checking out our underpants while we were wearing them.

Watching while I slept.

For at least one respondent, there was no possibility that her mother was watching out of concern and caring:

Watching while I had sex with my father.

Daughters Forced to Watch Mothers

Some of these mothers likely had a poor sense of what might be proper or healthy, but others were clearly exhibitionists, given that most of these events took place in a time when people were less "open" about innocent nakedness or bodily functions. Some reported their fathers also had poor boundaries in this area. Respondents report being made to watch their mothers expose themselves to the respondent or others (48%), dress or undress (47%), go to the bathroom (45%), bathe or shower (38%), masturbate (16%), or have sex (15%).

> She had no boundaries. She never closed the bathroom door. I wasn't so much compelled to watch as afraid to leave. She engaged me in conversation. She would walk around naked feeling herself out.

> [Watching her] dress and undress. I don't recall being made to "watch." I just did.

> She once masturbated while I had to watch her.

> Once my father attempted to [or did] have sex with her when I was in bed with them.

> Being made to watch her masturbate by my "other mother" (her female lover).

> Mother didn't usually wear underwear, therefore she was often exposed to all of us when we passed her bedroom or as she sat. She wore short gowns that were usually up as we passed by. She often requested my help in fastening her bra which she usually put on <u>after</u> I entered the room. She would continue to dry herself, even between her legs, while I waited to fasten her bra. I felt held prisoner and scared. For whatever reason I had the job of washing her underwear by hand even when she had her menses.

> Both my brothers and I were made to watch her change her Kotex — many, many times.

> Being made to watch her and my father dress and undress, bathe and shower, go to the bathroom, expose themselves, made to bathe with them, and helped him masturbate. He and she were always naked in warm weather.

93

Some of these mothers were clearly exhibitionists who used their daughters to satisfy their sexual desires.

Daughters Forced to Touch / Fondle Mothers

Forty-two percent (42%) of daughters report being made to sleep with their mothers, and 21% report being made to bathe with their mothers. Others report other forced intimacies such as being made to fondle their mothers' breasts (29%), vagina (29%), clitoris (25%), nipples (19%), lips (7%), rectum (4%), mouth (3%), anus (3%), or another part of the body (19%).

[I remember] Being made to lay in bed with her on weekend mornings.

She asked me often to rub her back, head or hair to help her sleep.

[I had to] wash her breasts.

Starting to remember fondling her breasts and nipples.

I washed her pelvic area with warm washcloths after she urinated, while she was still on the toilet.

[I was] made to fondle her legs and ass.

The operative words here are *made* and *fondle*. For example, during childhood, most children touch their mothers' breasts and may remember that experience with pleasure. What these daughters are reporting is something quite different, often remembered with revulsion. This physical contact *eroticized normal intimacy* between the child and her mother. This sexualization of intimacy has a long-term, devastating impact on the daughters.

Some of this elicited touching could be innocent, but much of it seems aimed at meeting the mothers' needs and not the children's. Respondents wrote:

[I had to] kiss scars from operations. I was made to fondle her body. She has trained my sister to use a vibrator on her joints and back and to give her hip manipulations, etc.

[She would] be sick all the time and [I was] made to sleep with her when she was sick.

Some reports may give rise to questions when the activity reported as abusive is something as apparently innocent as a mother asking for a back rub. How did the mother act during it? What tone of voice did she use to ask? How trapped and manipulated did the daughter feel?

Some daughters reported that they were required to do specific grooming tasks for their mothers:

[Squeeze] Blackheads on her neck and back. Yuck! Yuck!

Sexualized Touching of Mothers by Daughters

Some daughters reported touching was unquestionably sexual. Other respondents reported activities that were clearly for the mother's sexual gratification. Memories of such violations are often profoundly disturbing. Some daughters remember their mothers breathing heavily, feeling trapped against their mothers' bodies or feeling smothered. Some experience deep revulsion at such memories.

There can be a tremendous sense of betrayal by their own bodies in those who experienced pleasure or sexual excitement with their mothers. Some felt power in making their mothers' bodies respond sexually, but many others felt overwhelmed and overstimulated. One daughter reported she thought her mother was dead after orgasms.

This absence of boundaries and interacting of bodies may create a daughter's deep rejection of body features that resemble her mother's, and such revulsion may be generalized to the entire body. In addition, the daughters may feel revulsion for their mothers' bodies and touch. They wrote:

[I remember being made to] lay on top of her and under her.

Rubbing of our bodies together.

I did oral sex on her.

95

Being made to have oral sex with her, lick her genitals, and suck her nipples.

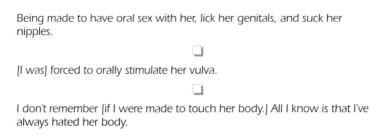

[I was] forced to orally stimulate her vulva.

I don't remember [if I were made to touch her body.] All I know is that I've always hated her body.

It's not surprising that when asked if she had been made to fondle her mother's body, one respondent simply said:

No, thank God!

Women must often work at being accepted as separate individuals, and that often means creating emotional distance from their mothers. Enmeshment with mothers is normal during *early* childhood, but many of these daughters had to fight for the survival of their true selves long afterward. At the physical and sexual level for them, it may still be a struggle to avoid feeling overwhelmed by their mothers. The following comment expresses this struggle in a remarkably direct way:

She used my body to rub hers ... tried to force it [mine] into hers.

Imagine the difficulty for a young woman of developing a healthy sense of female self when her mother had forced the girl's face, mouth, hands or even feet into the mother's body. Imagine, if you were a girl, what it would be like if you could not stop her from forcing herself into your body.

MOTHERS AND OTHERS:
MULTIPLE AND/OR JOINT PERPETRATION

Unfortunately, the survey included few questions about additional perpetrators. However, some patterns did emerge:

The role of co-perpetrator should not be minimized or discounted.

Approximately 70% of the daughters reported that *someone in addition to their mothers* sexually abused them. Sexual abuse by a mother, therefore, may be a predictor of multiple victimization of a child.

Sexual Abuse of Daughter by Father or "Other Parent"

Approximately 25% to 30% of the daughters informally reported that their fathers had also sexually abused them. The percentage may have been higher if a direct question had been asked as part of the survey. Clearly, those volunteering wanted others to know:

> I was also physically and sexually abused by my biological father.

> My abuse by my mother included abuse of me as an infant and also incidents when she actively encouraged my father to abuse me in her presence. One of your questions directly approaches the possibility of mother-father acting in collusion in abuse, which is the situation with its own dynamic and tragic consequences.

> I was abused by both parents — there's nothing written about this.

> I was sexually abused by my mother in the presence of my father who was also abusing me. How many women were sexually abused by both?

Each abuser may hide such abuse from the other perpetrator(s). Some daughters indicated their parents both knew and were protective of each other.

> I was also physically and sexually abused by my father. I remember one time they were together; otherwise my parents kept it secret from each other.

> [I remember her] watching while I had sex with my father.

> The husband [if also a perpetrator] may also cover up for the wife.

There may be more families where both parents sexually abuse children than previously realized. And we have to accept that in some cases the mother may be more sexually aggressive and may have been the initiator of the abuse behavior. Mathews et al. (1989) indicate that some women became sexually abusive after abuse was first initiated by a male, but this does not always seem to be the case. In addition, some parents abuse their daughters separately from one another. This dual abuse may make it difficult for the daughters to determine the impact of each parent's abuse. This kind of double dose is horribly destructive for the child.

> It is hard to separate out what were/are responses to the incest with mom and the incest with dad.

Some daughters are equally enraged at their abusive fathers.

> I question how devastating the effects of this abuse [by my mother] was on me, considering that my father betrayed me so awfully. I know I <u>hate</u> my father and can feel the effects [of the abuse] specifically, but with my mother it's harder to <u>name</u> and localize the effects. There's more deep pain in my gut which would destroy the world if it ever came out.

In my view, the cost of such rage through life is enormous.

Some offending fathers may themselves have a history of childhood sexual abuse or emotional domination by females. Some of the fathers may have found sexual excitement and arousal in the daughters' forced submission to the mothers' abuse, in the actual sexual activity, or even in the dominance by the mothers. Some of the fathers were clearly sexually aggressive or opportunistic, although others were more voyeuristic and passive. Some may find sexual relief, excitement and/or safety through seeing a child dominated by a female. Some may be sexually aroused by the secretiveness of the mother's sexual activities.

A few abusive mothers also acted as "sexual providers" by instigating sexual activity and abuse between the child and others, including the fathers. Some of this "providing" may be connected to the sexual dysfunction of the mother, the father, or both.

One respondent reported that she felt abused by both her mother and her mother's female lover who was like a second parent and lived next door:

> The "other mother" would put her fingers in my vagina while my mother would use the enema. I was told if I didn't go to the bathroom I would be very sick. After a long period of time it did feel good. My mother would work the enema in and out telling me I had to be clean all inside. I didn't like the soap and water going in.

Sexual Activities with Others in Mothers' Presence

The survey asked about performance of sex acts with the mother present, but not directly involved:

Q. Were you made to …	Yes	No	Unsure
Take part in sexual activities with others while mother watched?	26%	65%	9%
Take part in ritualized sexual activities with her and others?	15%	70%	2%

These responses mean that at least one quarter (26%) or more of these mothers knew that someone else was sexually abusing their daughters. This knowledge reflects a profound lack of protection by the mothers. We far too easily assume that mothers protect their children.

> I was also molested by a woman friend of the family at around the same age (2). I'm not sure if I told [my mother]. There was also abuse by a male neighbor at age 6. My mother claims no knowledge of the woman having abused me but does confirm that she was a family friend at the time.

> [I was] concurrently abused by others.

Unfortunately, this study did not gather data on who took part in these activities, but based on my clinical experience with sexual abuse survivors, I suspect it was most often other family members, especially fathers, mothers' brothers, and/or the mothers' boyfriends.

Two respondents specifically mentioned a cult or activities typically thought of as cult abuse in explaining who else abused them:

> I was abused by adults who took part in a satanic, ritualistic abuse which included a medical doctor.

> I was abused while others watched and my animals were killed.

Being abused by multiple perpetrators makes it difficult for daughters to define the impact of each perpetrator later.

> I found it hard to see and describe my mother's abuse and the effects of it separate from abuse by my father and several others.

> Separating the incest with multiple perpetrators is difficult for me.

MULTI-GENERATIONAL ASPECTS OF FEMALE SEXUAL ABUSE

Multi-generational sexual abuse is likely transmitted along the female lines in some families. Several daughters reported their maternal grandmothers were sexually abusive of them. It is naïve for us to believe that women are incapable of passing on abusive patterns to the next generation of women.

> [I was] also sexually abused by my father and grandmother.

One respondent reported being made to watch her grandmother dress and undress, expose herself, to sleep with her, and to physically fondle her grandmother's clitoris and vagina. She also was made to engage in seductive behaviors and activities with her grandmother.

These daughters often feel the sexual abuse by mother is a core issue for them to resolve and that it was the forerunner to their other abuse experiences. In addition, it is not uncommon for the daughters to initially focus on abuse by someone other than their mothers.

> It is very hard to accept, to blame a "mother" or to name her as the abuser. [It's] much easier with others.

> Having been abused by both my mother and father as well as many others, [I know sexual abuse by mother] is far more emotionally damaging and is harder to deal with in therapy and to get over.

THE GROWING CHILD: ADOLESCENT ABUSE EXPERIENCES

Adolescence is a critical developmental stage when children begin to move away from their family circle and into peer groups. They make a normal leap towards independence as a surge of hormones focuses their attention on their bodies and sexuality. This survey did not ask specific questions about the daughters' adolescent abuse experiences, but many wrote comments about this turbulent period of their lives.

When the Nightmare Does Not Stop: Effects of Continued Sexual Abuse in Daughters' Adolescence

The findings of this survey indicate a pattern of increased psychiatric problems and/or psychiatric hospitalizations among daughters whose mothers continued the sexual abuse into the daughters' adolescence. Several of these daughters were later hospitalized or institutionalized, some repeatedly. They tended to report more serious diagnoses than other adolescents and were prescribed a wider range of medications. Sexual abuse by a mother during adolescence may cause a dramatic and devastating collapse of a daughter's ability to defend her person and ego. She may then, for example, appear schizophrenic enough to be diagnosed and mistakenly treated as if she *were* schizophrenic, including being hospitalized and medicated.

Sexual abuse by a mother during a daughter's teen years may also interfere with the social and emotional passage into adulthood. Any continuing pull on the daughters towards emotional and sexual fusion with the mother may make the daughter feel as if she's failed to achieve the transition into adulthood, as one respondent notes:

It's difficult to draw a line between childhood and adult life. At 28 I've only now come to realize it was sexual abuse [even though] it didn't start until I was 14 or 15. It was covert and not obviously sexual.

If mother/daughter fusion persists into late adolescence or adulthood, it may include shared mental illness. The daughter may end up bearing and expressing the external signs and symptoms of such shared mental illness (especially paranoia) though the mother carefully keeps her symptoms hidden. The original fusion may then be disguised as parental concern for the daughter's disturbed or collapsed emotional condition.

This daughter expressed how damaging sexual abuse by a mother can be to her teen daughter.

Maternal abuse is the most difficult for the victim to face, I think. It's the most likely to be repressed and never surface. Also if it is in consciousness I believe it could lead to schizophrenic psychosis — especially in teenage girls as a way of defending against the reality of the abuse.

True schizophrenia derives from other causes but this respondent is pointing out the potential for severe psychiatric impact caused by such abuse during adolescence, including psychotic reactions. The responses to this survey show that when sexual abuse by mothers continues into the daughters' adolescence, the rate of adult psychiatric problems and/or adult psychiatric hospitalizations among the daughters rises.

Such crises are caused in part by a daughter's need to become an individual and separate from her mother. When the mothers don't stop the abuse, the teen daughter must struggle with a constant threat of being pulled backwards towards continued enmeshment with her mother as sexual boundaries are crossed and recrossed. As the daughters grew older, they may have had to cope with new levels of awareness about the experiences they had.

Increased Ability to Name the Abuse During Adolescence

During their teens, many daughters became aware of the damage being done to them by the abuse. In childhood, they might not have understood quite what was happening, but if the abuse continued into their teen years, they knew. Some wrote:

> Not all of mothers' touching is caretaking and nurturing. The mother that forces her 13 year old daughter's face to brush her teeth for her because she can't do it right is just as invasive, intrusive, and controlling as the mother who invades her teenage daughter's shower to show her how to scrub her "privates" correctly! I've met these grown up children who are just as damaged as the daughters who were screwed by their fathers!

> While my primary abuse by my mother was physical, it had sexual overtones which I only became aware of later…removing my underpants for a spanking at 14 years of age…spanking me in front of mirror so she could watch. The sexual nature of the abuse may be more subtle than overt fondling or sexual stimulation.

> The sexual and physical abuse seemed separate. She did both. Except forcing me to lie across the bed to receive whippings until 13 years of age.

For some daughters, there was a constant threat of sexual boundaries being crossed.

> After the abuse had stopped she would wait until I was in the bath tub and then come in and go to the bathroom and stay until I got out. [She would also watch me while I defecated] if she got the chance.

The next respondent noted her mother's actions caused confusion for both the daughter and son, whether he understood it or not.

As a young teen she didn't want me to shave my legs and armpits but encouraged my brother to do so!?!? He's a "closet transvestite" as an adult. Do you think there is a connection? Betcha!!

CHAPTER 8

Related to the Pain:
Additional Aspects of Abuse

T here are wide-ranging additional aspects of sexual abuse reflected in these daughters' experiences. The survey asked about such aspects as the ages of both abusers and the children they abused; the time, place and duration of the abuse in the respondents' lives; nuances of emotional abuse, including seduction-like behaviors; accompanying physical abuse; and the daughters' responses.

AGE AND DURATION

Mothers Old and Young:
Mothers' Ages During Active Abuse

According to the daughters' reports, the mothers' average age when the abuse began was 32 years old. Their average age when the abuse ended was 40.6 years old.

The youngest mother at start of abuse was 25 years old, and the oldest mother started abusing her daughter when she was 51 years old. The youngest mother to stop abusing the respondent daughter was 32 years old, and the oldest to cease her abuse was 53 years old. One daughter noted:

> I believe the abuse occurred during her mid-40's.

The reports of these daughters on their mothers' ages reflect an older age range than is seen in other female sex-offender studies. In those studies, teenagers and young adult women were found most often to be the offenders, and much of the activity was exploratory in nature. The mothers in this study were older, tended to be married, had already been sexual, given that they were the victims' mothers, and the abuse often went on for a long period of time.

When It All Began: Survivors' Ages at Abuse Onset

The *average* daughter's age when the abuse began was 3.2 years old. One respondent added:

> [I believe it began] when I was born and continues in her mind [and mine!].

This number is disturbing. On the survey, the daughters were asked to manually write their ages, rather than simply checking off an age category. So while the ages of onset listed here are shockingly young, they also indicate very conscious responses by the daughters (the percentages reported here are cumulative): 18% report that they were under 1 year old when the abuse began; 60% were under 2 years old; 78% were under 5 years old; 90% were under 8 years old.

The implications of such occurrences at these young ages are staggering. How could there not be a damaging impact from these daughters' experiences?

> Some of my earliest memories are ones of sexual abuse. At least as early as age 3 or 4 both my parents were sexually abusive in overt and covert ways. They stripped me, looked at me, and made me watch them engage in sexual acts. The most frequent kind of occurrence that I remember is that they laid me on the kitchen table, gave me enemas, and rubbed me between my legs. At least some of the time I had orgasms and they continued to stimulate me. I experienced this as torture.

I am not sure about this. I was 2½ when it started and I don't have all the memories.

Probably 99% of toddlers' lives may be hidden by parents from public scrutiny except for very blatant abuse. Could there be a much more vulnerable victim? One respondent reports:

My mother began abusing me physically and sexually after I was raped by an uncle. It was as if the abuse was punishment for getting raped. I was 2½ years old.

Consider what girls of five or younger cannot do. They cannot seduce anyone. They do not have the power to make anyone mentally ill or to ruin anyone's life. They cannot make any adult drink too much alcohol. Most importantly, they cannot be appropriate sexual partners for any responsible adult. Yet at very young ages, these respondent daughters were burdened with a terrible legacy to resolve and understand, or, as often happens, to try to bury, forget, and hide.

Unable to Speak about the Unspeakable: Preverbal Abuse

Preverbal abuse is a critical issue in many mother-daughter sexual abuse cases. The ability of a child to think, observe, narrate, remember, and recount rises dramatically between ages three and six. The data indicate that about 80% of these 93 respondents had been sexually abused by their mothers before they were old enough to understand and/or narratively recall what was occurring. These sexual offenses often occurred before the daughters were old enough to speak about what was happening or put words to the experience as cognitive language. Therefore, the abuse was frequently not stored as having mental meaning but as physical sensations.

Some daughters may not have stored clear, concise memories of separate abusive incidents but rather as vague physical and emotional feelings. Perhaps later they disliked being touched in certain ways, or being touched by their mothers or by women in general. They may feel overstimulated and uncomfortable sometimes and not know why.

This does not mean that every unexplained discomfort someone experiences is a veiled symptom of sexual abuse. Adults must determine for themselves if that might be the case. However, the results of the survey indicate that many women may have been sexually stimulated at very young ages.

How Long Did the Mothers Abuse?

The average length of time the daughters were abused by their mothers was 8.5 to 10 years. The daughters ranged in age during the abuse from infancy to 61 years old (the 61-year-old daughter reports that her mother was still fondling her at the time of the survey).

The shortest abuse period reported was one time to over one year. The longest abuse period reported was 18 years. As one daughter added:

> It stopped after two years when I was 6 or 7 years old. But then more people started.

Many respondents made a distinction between overt, direct sexual abuse and covert or non-touch sexual abuse.

> Most of the overt abuse ended early [age 5] but the verbal, more covert sexual abuse continued longer.

The daughters report that as they grew older, the sexual abuse often became less physical and directly sexual, but more verbal or voyeuristic. If it did not end quickly, it was apt to be a prolonged involvement:

> The sexual abuse by my mother continued covertly my entire life until I told her to leave me alone. Her contacts with me since then still have the lover-like attitude and make me sick. I told someone 33 years after it began. But the nature of my abuse was a warp in the entire relationship, not a sexual event — many events. It would still be going on if I was in contact with her.

> I was an adult [during some of it]. The abuse continued until I was 24 and still continues on a verbal level.

When Did it End?
Daughters' Ages When the Abuse Stopped

The daughters' average age when the abuse ended was 17.3 years old, and they ranged in age from infancy to 56 years old when the abuse ended (as noted, in at least one case the sexual contact was still ongoing, i.e., did not end). In cumulative terms, approximately one quarter (26%) were 10 and under, 48% were 16 and under, and three quarters (76%) were 23 and under when it ended.

In the beginning of this research, it was assumed that there could be a clear distinction between sexual abuse and other forms of abuse by the mothers. However, the data discussed so far and the comments below reveal the extent to which the sexual abuse was also often emotionally abusive and any emotional abuse was highly sexualized. The actual physical/sexual abuse often ended by the time the daughters reached adolescence.

[I was 10] when the physical abuse stopped but the other abuse continued.

Some mothers continued their abusive behaviors as long as they could, as one respondent wrote:

It hasn't stopped except that I asked my mom not to contact me. When she does she still perpetrates.

Emotional [abuse] continued until my mother's death when I was 28.

One daughter reports a successful confrontation with her mother while in elementary school:

She stopped abusing me when I told her it was wrong and I wouldn't touch her. I was raped by her brother around then.

Unfortunately, there were many other perpetrators during this survivor's early life.

Non-Abusive Periods

When asked if there were periods within the abusive time span when there was no abuse, 59% of the daughters answered yes, 29% said no, and 11% were unsure. Some added comments:

A couple of weeks here and there.

Mostly it was a daily thing.

It sometimes appeared difficult for a survivor to know clearly what non-abusive periods were like or if there were any:

I don't know. I can't remember. The abuse with my mother and my alcoholic uncle happened during the same 2-to-3-year time span and in the same house. It was intermittent with him and I don't remember with her.

In the face of any continuing threat, many daughters did what the next respondent did, once they became old enough:

I kept moving farther away.

No Safe Places:
Where Sexual Abuse Occurred

Many of the survey respondents were sexually abused in what can be considered the "female" parts of the home: 75% took place in a bedroom, 58% in the bathroom, 21% in the kitchen and 20% in the living room of the homes. The survey offered a variety of other selections, but the percentages drop drastically after those locations: 7% in a closet; 5% outdoors; 4% in an automobile; 3% in the garage; 2% in a relative's home; 2% in the dining room; 1% in the mother's workplace; and 1% in a tent.

Twelve (12) other locations were mentioned by individual respondents. Eight (8) of the daughters (8.6%) mentioned being abused in basements and/or attics:

[I was abused in a] locked room in our basement.

Two percent (2%) reported being sexually abused in cemeteries and 2% in churches. Others noted places such as a warehouse and an abandoned house. Some abuse occurred in supposedly "safe" places for children, such as a store changing room, a doctor's office, and at summer camp. Two daughters noted:

In my crib.

[It happened] next door at my other mother's house [who was my mother's lover].

VIOLENCE, AGGRESSION, AND SEDUCTION IN MOTHER-DAUGHTER ABUSE

The daughters were asked to indicate on a five-point scale ("(a) Violent; (b); (c) Mixed; (d); (e) Lover") which letter location best described how their mothers related to them at the time of the abuse.

Choice "(a)" in answer to questions about violent sexual abuse was described on the survey instrument as "abusive/violent: she acted out her frustrations, rage, confusion on me." Thirty percent (30%), the largest proportion of daughters, chose this, the option of greatest violence on the scale. Another 19% chose "(b)" the next most violent position, for a total of 49% (nearly half) of the daughters reporting that their experience of sexual abuse was also physically violent. If we add in the 21% who indicated their abuse was a mixture of violence and seductive/lover-like behavior (choice "(c)"), we find a total of 70% who say there was some degree of physical violence along with their sexual abuse. We must remember that this behavior began, on average, when the daughters were 3.2 years of age.

Some of the daughters report brutal assaults and/or torture.

> My mother threatened to burn my hair/me if I did not comply. I was given beer to drink. I was beaten and there were threats that I would be burned if I wasn't quiet. Sometimes I was slightly burned on the buttocks with lit cigarettes. I learned not to cry and to stop screaming. Sometimes I remember these experiences as ones that I witnessed from across the room. Most of the time my mother did this sort of thing to me alone. Other times my father was involved as well. They also inserted objects into my vagina and/or rectum. My mother at least once made me lick her vulva and touch her anus. She showed me a lit safety match and threatened to burn the hair off my head if I didn't do it.

Some of the sexual assaults may have been re-enactments of sexual abuse in the mother's past, and some mothers were violent as a part of the overall mother/child relationship.

> [I was] raped by her with the addition of [having my] ankles tied, mouth taped and blindfolded.

> My mother was never sexually abusive towards me in a violent way but was violent in her physical abuse.

A second survey question focused specifically on physical abuse that accompanied the sexual abuse (for example: hitting, being tied, objects placed in body). Asked about physical/sexual abuse in this manner, 65% of the daughters said yes, it had been part of the abuse they experienced, 22% said no, and 13% said they were unsure. These numbers are consistent with the combined 70% noted above. Some added comments:

> It was very sadistic, violent and painful.

> [I suffered] traumatic, painful, physical abuse.

These reports must be taken seriously. Some daughters feel they were "targeted" by their mothers.

> There was more of an angry, punishing aspect to the abuse than sexual. Although her repressed sexuality did "leak" out on to me, I felt more like I was a receptacle of her rage.

It is important to understand the capacity for violence in some of these mothers. There were reports of occurrences that frankly qualify as torture, while other daughters in this study were near death from their abuse. A few respondents do not know how they lived through their childhoods. Such extreme abuse is deeply troubling and often difficult to talk about and remember.

> I have never had any sexual contact with my mother that was not violent and painful and full of rage on her part. Most victims I know say that is not true for them. I'd be interested in statistics on that.

This respondent sample may include a higher number of violently sexually abused daughters than found in a random sample of sexually abused daughters. Some respondents took part in the survey because they had read *When You're Ready* which describes physically violent sexual abuse. Some may have been more willing to reveal such abuse assuming that I would understand. In fact, those reporting incidents on the more violent end of the scale gave the fullest disclosure of their experiences. However, even if this particular survey is slightly skewed, with more violence reported than actually occurs, until and unless this level of physical violence is proven false, these data should be taken very seriously.

Violent Sexual Abuse Mixed with Seduction

The middle choice, (c), was described on the survey as "a mixture of aggression and seduction." This form of abuse may link physical aggression and sexuality together for the daughters at very young ages.

[She gave me] spankings [which] sometimes gave me orgasms.

There was guilt, anxiety, fear that something was going on but Mother was a good person.

Forced confinement was common in the physical abuse. Two respondents described details:

I was tied to my bed [arms and legs] as a toddler. She says it was only to keep me out of trouble early in the A.M.

Once [she] tied [my] legs to the kitchen table.

The Seduction of a Child:
Sexual Abuse with Seductive Behaviors

Choice "(e)" was described on the survey instrument as "I was a substitute lover. She used me to act out her sexual fantasies and needs. Seductive but not violent."

Eighteen percent (18%) chose this position on the scale, indicating that the sexual abuse by their mothers was primarily lover-like and seductive. If position (d) is added, the total is 27%; if the mixed category is added, the total is 48%.

There were fewer survivor comments about the lover-type relationships, and this sexual abuse by mothers may be more often concealed by the daughters. I suspect that this survey design did not reach this group as well as those who had experienced violence. This group warrants additional extensive research, however, as, clearly, the seductive sexual abuse by mothers had strong impacts.

I slept in my mother's bed from the time I was born and was given enemas regularly for many years. I have recently come to realize that I perceive my mother to have been my first lover. I have had no lovers since although I have been married twice and have two children.

113

This form of abuse may be very difficult for the daughters to stop and for others to understand.

> The most important aspect of the abuse I experienced was the insidiousness of it and how all-pervasive it was. My mother was obsessed with me, with every aspect of my physical appearance, hygiene and development. She continued in treating me as a lover, talking to me as if I was her lover, buying my underwear for me, buying identical sleepwear and blouses to hers, finding reasons to see me in the nude — on through my adult life.

Other questions asked if the daughters recalled being made to engage in seductive behaviors, activities and/or games with their mothers: 43% answered yes, 44% said no, and 3% answered that they were unsure. These numbers confirm the daughters' characterization of the abuse as "mixed" to seductive and lover-like.

There is reason to speculate that the seductive, lover-like relationships are often deeply rooted, prolonged, and emotionally entrapping for the participants. The mother and daughter bond in these relationships may be powerful and sexual. The mothers may attempt some level of sexual contact long after the child is grown and make it a condition of a continued relationship.

> She still does! She's 69 years old! She acts coy and seductive and talks about [her] sexual activity with my father!! Even if I don't want to hear it.

Violations of Mind and Body:
Emotional, Physical, and Sexual Abuse

Many daughters report a mixture of sexual, physical, verbal and emotional abuse. A typical pattern is for all four forms of abuse to begin during pre-school years and continue until early adolescence. Emotional and verbal forms are the most apt to continue into the daughter's adulthood.

> [It has continued] my entire life [of 48 years]. Physical abuse happened between ages 1–2 and the sexual abuse ages 1 to 5. The emotional abuse never stopped.

> She is still emotionally and verbally abusive at times, and is now 54 years old. But the actual physical abuse was limited to under six months. The more subtle sexual abuse like neglecting to explain things, exhibiting herself, sexual comments, etc., went on longer.

These multiple forms of abuse may create confusion when the daughter tries to understand the overall family dynamics.

> I think trying to [define or] limit abuse to certain time frames may be misleading in that some physical activity may come and go but the familial atmosphere is unlikely to have changed so that I expect the "abuse" is more chronic and ongoing than implied by the question "when did it start and stop?"

In one part of the survey the daughters were asked if they experienced emotional pain or discomfort with the sexual abuse (for example, fear, being told scary things, and being made to feel bad, sinful, or dirty). Ninety percent (90%) answered yes, 2% said no, and 8% wrote that they were unsure. This is an alarmingly high rate of emotional pain. The emotional abuse often starts early, perhaps at the very beginning of the sexual abuse, and remains a problem long after the sexual and/or physical abuse ends.

> [The] emotional abuse feels worse than the sexual abuse.

> This survey centers on sexual abuse and its effect. In my experience the sexual abuse was followed by physical and mental abuse as I grew older and could resist sexual abuse. She would do scary things like hide in a closet and pull me in.

> The emotional abuse has never stopped. As of today she is nearly 70 years old. It's just plain hatred at being alive.

Some mothers project their own childhood traumas onto their daughters, and their long-term emotional abuse of the daughters may keep their own sexual trauma externalized. Having sexually abused their daughters, the mothers can then deposit on them the burden of being the victim in their place. The daughters then represent the "bad/damaged-goods/less-than-whole" feelings within the mothers. In emotional abuse, it is possible for the mothers to project these kinds of emotions and feeling outward onto daughters. The emotional abuse may also enforce low family status on the daughters and relieve those feelings in the mothers. An abusive mother's pain may thus be transferred to a daughter.

> The tie-in between sexual and emotional abuse seems important. I know I was given many examples of my "badness" before, during, and after the sexual abuse.

It is impossible to overstate how pervasive and overwhelming emotional abuse can be from some of the highly dysfunctional mothers. It is also clear that some of the abuse was deliberately tormenting and destructive.

> I find it impossible to isolate the incest from the context of the overall emotionally abusive relationship.

> The abuse was more than a series of events; it was a context.

These mothers have total access to the child and the ability to hide the abuse, often with the collusion of family and society. When the sexual abuse diminishes, the emotional abuse may become relentless.

PAINFUL RESPONSES
TO A CONFUSING REALITY

The daughters' own responses to the sexual abuse, the seductive atmosphere, or other enmeshing aspects of their mothers' relationships with them can be a powerful source of emotional pain both in their child-hood and now as adults. Two specific responses were explored in this study: feeling "special" because of the sexual abuse; and sexual arousal or physical pleasure during the sexually abusive activities.

Feeling Special Because of the Abuse

Thirty-one percent (31%) of the daughters reported that the sexual abuse made them feel special during childhood. However, this response may give the child a distorted view of herself and cause other problems in adulthood, in a dynamic that could be considered an aspect of emotional abuse. One daughter commented:

> This has passed with my mom, but I have transferred it to other relationships, especially with female authority figures.

Survivor Arousal or Pleasure from the Sexual Abuse

The daughters were asked if at times there was pleasure in the sexual activity with their mothers. Thirty-nine percent (39%) said yes, 33% said no, and 20% were unsure. One daughter added:

[Yes], whether I want to admit it or not.

Many daughters are repulsed by the idea of sexual arousal or pleasure from activities with their mothers:

Are you kidding? Ugh!

Definitely not!

NEVER!!!

Yet children are physically capable of responding to sexual stimulation. One respondent previously quoted indicated that she had orgasms when spanked. Another wrote, *"After a while it did feel good,"* referring to enemas combined with digital stimulation.

[I experienced] sexual tension and arousal [from the abuse].

One comment suggested that the resulting excitement had to be either contained or discharged somewhere:

[I kept getting] intense crushes on little girls. [And I] sexualized relationships with adult women [e.g., teachers]. I masturbated the dog!? This all started EARLY!

Any similar leaking or discharge of the sexual stimulation may be remembered with embarrassment or shame in later years. However, the anatomy and physical mechanisms with which to be sexually responsive are in place during childhood. Self-stimulation is a common response to sexual abuse as a child.

As a child there were times I couldn't stop masturbating.

Children have few appropriate outlets for the sexual energy that has been awakened in them by abuse. Children are frequently presented in sexualized ways in advertising and entertainment yet as a society we do not expect children to be sexual.

If an individual has not yet explored (or felt safe enough to explore) her own responses, it may make it difficult to hear the experiences of others who do remember sexual pleasure. Others are clear they may have felt sexual stimulation or arousal, but they apparently don't view it as pleasurable.

I'm not aware of any.

I was physically stimulated by my sister touching me and also by my mother parading around naked but I would never call it "pleasure."

There is deep conflict when the daughters feel sexually stimulated by their mothers' touch when what they really want to experience is nurturing touch.

It was the only time she <u>sometimes</u> touched me gently.

Acknowledging such sexual pleasure forces the daughters to recognize that abuse did occur and that their mothers were not like the stereotypical mother. There is often a deep sense that something is wrong with them if there were any sexual pleasure. They may feel betrayed by their bodies' responses, believe they were "disturbed," or that their "inner children" are perverse and disturbed. Such pleasure is often wholly unthinkable.

I attach shame to that pleasure and profound embarrassment.

They may remain silent and fearful of the reactions of others and are left with a reality and memories for which there is no social language, no common imagery, and perhaps no outlet. The phrase "sexual with my mother" is a social oxymoron.

It is not comfortable for child victims to be repeatedly sexually stimulated and passively remain the container of someone else's sexual aggression. Nineteen percent (19%) of the daughters convinced themselves, therefore, that they were active and equal partners in the sexual abuse.

Taking responsibility. It was me.

Given the daughters' average age of three when the abuse began, it is virtually impossible that they were truly equal sexual partners, especially in the beginning of the abuse. Some daughters may have been taught to initiate sexual activity with their mothers. Some children attempt to balance power by sexually engaging others, including animals, who are less powerful. Such behavior is almost always connected to a perpetrator's violation of them.

In survivor circles, sexual pleasure and orgasms during the abuse are seldom mentioned. Orgasms with one's mother seems a nearly taboo subject. One of the contributions of these study participants is their bravery and honesty in statements like these that might help open up this topic:

> No, [there wasn't pleasure with my mother] but there was in the activity with my uncle, a seductive abuser. This was a terribly difficult issue to work through. I see it as another well-kept secret, even in survivors' groups.

The large majority of respondents indicate that there was no pleasure in the abuse by mothers; this exploration of it as a taboo topic yet a valid occurrence should not be misconstrued as suggesting anything different. It's a subject that some survivors need to explore; as clinicians, we must help make it safe to do that. The pleasure discussed here should *not* be confused with chosen, adult, sexual pleasure. I've never met or heard from a survivor of sexual abuse by her mother who was not conflicted by the experience.

Part Four

THE EFFECTS OF SEXUAL ABUSE BY MOTHERS

CHAPTER 9

Long-Term Harm:
Daughters' Damage

We now have a clearer picture of what these mothers did that their daughters experienced as abusive. Some people — therapy professionals, social workers and others may still question what harm was really done.

The daughters were asked to grade damage from the abuse on a five-point scale. *All of the daughters* (100%) believe the sexual abuse was damaging. This finding cannot be overstated. Twenty-seven percent (27%) of the respondents indicated the abuse was damaging but hope for a full recovery. Seventy-three percent (73%) of the daughters reported feeling the most severe degrees of damage. These data are disturbing, and the lack of hope they express is troubling.

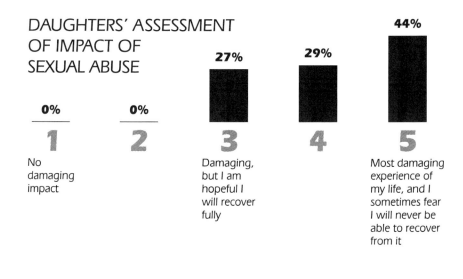

DAUGHTERS' ASSESSMENT OF IMPACT OF SEXUAL ABUSE

1	2	3	4	5
0%	0%	27%	29%	44%
No damaging impact		Damaging, but I am hopeful I will recover fully		Most damaging experience of my life, and I sometimes fear I will never be able to recover from it

Some study participants added comments:

> It's the ugliest, most repulsive thing I can think of. I feel so much shame. I hope I can overcome it.

> I <u>know</u> I won't [be free from its impact]!

> That's how it feels now. Hard to imagine that it would completely be O.K. But I hope so. I'm working on these issues and I'm committed to keeping at it until it's resolved.

Regarding recovery, one daughter expressed what many daughters probably feel:

> On any given day or hour this answer changes.

TIES THAT BIND: THE BONDS BETWEEN MOTHERS AND DAUGHTERS

Profound connections can be discovered in the sexual problems faced by these mothers and those reported by their daughters. One cannot examine these data for long without seeing the long-reaching effects these mothers have on many aspects of their daughters' lives.

The daughter literally emerges from her mother's body, survives through her care and feeding, and is influenced throughout life by the mother, even in her absence. Daughters may not like that reality, but it's true. Even if a mother dies at her daughter's birth, the daughter still inherits her mother's genes.

To some extent, society expects daughters to replicate their mothers' lives. Everyone can make choices, and some women are very different from their mothers; however, a mother's influence is profound, long-lasting and subtle.

Some mothers project their unresolved pain and confusion onto their children. Some project guilt, sexual confusion, anger and rage, a need for power, or the fear of sex and intimacy onto their daughters.

> This is where my understanding is at this point: I became an unwanted, unacceptable, despicable, rejected part of my mother. I believe she projected onto me a view/experience of herself as a "bad child" that she formed in response to her physically abusive father and rejecting mother. As a young child, she internalized her mother's rejection of her and her rage toward her father, and she came to dislike and doubt herself. As a young mother, she projected her self-loathing onto me: I became the ugly, worthless, death-deserving one.

Some of these mothers must feel they have, for better or worse, reproduced themselves through their daughters. These mothers may re-experience their childhood pain, ambivalence, and rage through contact with their daughters, their daughters' little girl bodies and vulnerability. Additionally, the daughters are exposed to their mothers' behaviors and emotional states, and maternal projection may be taken in without clarification, filtration or conscious choice by the daughters.

For example, a mother might feel sexually shamed and sinful and repeatedly project those feelings onto her daughter as a way to get them out of herself. The daughter may take those messages in as true about herself.

The aftermath of such relationships often includes problems in mental health, sexuality, substance abuse and possibly eating disorders. We cannot ignore that a major lesson in these relationships is how to numb emotions and avoid pain rather than resolve it.

WHOM TO LOVE: SEXUAL IDENTITY

Childhood Sexual Feelings

This abuse was, in fact, sexual in nature, and it created sexual excitement: 34% of the respondents reported childhood sexual excitement; 44% of the abused daughters engaged in childhood sexual self-stimulation; and 46% identified themselves as participating in childhood sexualized behaviors (for example, frequent masturbation, watching others, etc.).

[I experienced] sexual tension and arousal [from the abuse].

The children's sexual stimulation and arousal had to find release. Many of their sexual energies and behaviors were focused on themselves, and self-stimulation often began early, with a driven quality.

[I did] compulsive masturbation.

As a child, there were times I couldn't stop masturbating.

They may also have experienced a periodic return of sexual energies and their conscious awareness of sexuality.

I had 4 or 5 different ages (i.e. eight, thirteen, sixteen, and twenty-one years old) where I "learned" to masturbate. Each time I would have compulsive masturbation for a while and then stop and forget I had ever done it. Years later I now remember having learned it over and over. On at least one occasion, I started to have memories of the incest and that seems to be why I stopped.

Thirty-five percent (35%) of the daughters reported some early sexual acting-out behaviors that often involved sexual promiscuity. The adult survivors are often embarrassed by these childhood behaviors.

Fifteen percent (15%) of the respondents report that during childhood they sexually abused others. This activity likely involved sexual contact with children either their own age or younger. They may feel deeply that this makes them "just like my mother," even if what they actually did was normal childhood sexual exploration. Some of them likely did, however, engage in sexually abusive and aggressive behaviors, and self-reports of childhood abuse of other children should be taken seriously by professionals.

A few daughters report that they were sexually abusive or exploitive of animals during childhood: 10% of the daughters reported that they hurt animals in childhood, and 4% that they tortured or killed animals. Reports of these behaviors also should not be dismissed lightly by professionals. Children often invest human qualities in animals. The daughters' pets may have been the most loyal, consistent and loving beings in their lives, and they may feel deep shame for mistreating or taking advantage of those animals. Such violations can be painful for an adult to reveal. We have to understand how the animals became involved and the experiences that led to the abuse by the daughter.

> The most difficult part of the abuse by my mother was to face the truth about her teaching me to be sexual with cats and dogs. After 42 years of believing that I must have been a horribly psychologically sick child to have come up with that idea all by myself. I had to struggle for many years to break free of that addiction to being sexual with animals since it was totally pleasurable and there were "no strings attached" sexually like there were with both my parents. The only guilt over the sex with animals is because of society's reaction to this form of sexual gratification. For me [as a child] it was safe and I didn't have to live up to anybody's expectations or try to meet their needs. I felt free, spontaneous and loved.

Adolescent Sexuality

During their teen years, as children begin to move out of the family circle and into peer groups, a surge of hormones focuses their attention on their bodies and sexuality. This survey did not ask about adolescent sexual issues, but many respondents wrote about it. By adolescence, they often had become acutely aware of the implications of their same-sex experiences and of homophobia in others. During their teens, some respondents began to act out.

> After age 12 I suppressed my sexual feels unless I was drunk. [I did] prostitution.

> [I became] extremely covert … hiding black boyfriends.

Dealing with their emerging sexuality was often like having to cross an emotional mine field.

> [I did] masturbation [with] intense guilt. But [it was] determination to be able to have guilt-free and happy orgasms. Used it as a "tool" to test my progress. Later (age 23 or so) I wondered if I [were] a lesbian.

All young people face new experiences and questions, but these daughters' emerging sexuality contained a deep and horrific secret. Developing sexual comfort and solid sexual identity often was delayed or incomplete until adulthood.

For example, many young people consider the possibility that they are homosexual. For these daughters, the sexual abuse by their mothers may make them deeply troubled by such thoughts. Abuse by their mothers may block the freedom to fully consider and resolve issues of sexual identity, boundary setting, power in relationships, or to explore what does and doesn't give them pleasure. Some feel "sexually stuck." Some daughters cannot be emotionally or physically present during sex. Many repress their sexuality entirely.

Adult Sexuality

Eight-two percent (82%) of the daughters reported sexual problems in adulthood. The issues of basic physical and/or sexual functioning can be painful. The 93 daughters in this study reported that 73% of them had problems being sexual; 69% of the respondents felt sexual nervousness; and 33% of them experienced over-stimulation when sexual.

> It may affect your view of yourself as female. It may get in the way of your feeling like a grownup woman. It may affect your ability to be a sexual person.

> I had a "dead" clitoris until I was 35. I did not wash my genitals until I was 18. I did not masturbate or reach a climax (same occasion) until I was 25. I have to hold my body in a position so my clitoris will not be triggered by one of the hundreds of things throughout the day that might trigger it. My posture is terrible [because] I am constantly having to do this.

> I always feel like I have to pee. I'm always aware of that part of my physical functions. I react with sexual stimulation to <u>many</u> things, usually things that make me angry or that remind me of my mother and sister [perpetrator].

> [I feel I have] inappropriate sexual arousal over non-sexual stimulation or thoughts such as getting sexually aroused reading about enemas or hearing words implying threats and control. I feel I abused my infant son mildly.

When memories of sexual abuse by their mothers were repressed, the process of remembering had a major impact on some daughters. Some of the daughters report confusion and sexual dysfunction.

> [I] felt oversexed prior to the memories which surfaced and since [remembering], my sexual activity and desire has decreased substantially. I never thought I'd ever not want sex. Do enjoy cuddling and intimacy with my spouse. Thought I was just being more mature in my middle age, but now wonder if the memory was what changed it.

> At 37, I'm 13 years old sexually … and very confused … easier to be asexual.

> True sexuality is still a mystery to me although I was able to keep up an adequate pretense for many years.

These difficulties do not appear without reasons. One of the daughters quoted here reported that she was forced to perform oral sex on her mother and was also sexually abused by her father.

Some daughters experience issues related to freedom and the ability to function sexually and/or engage in certain sexual activities comfortably.

> I'm not sure if I performed oral sex on her [my mother], but I feel very scared and uneasy when I even think about that now. I'm very comfortably a lesbian and I'm in a long term, loving relationship which is better than I could have imagined having. But I can't do that with my partner. It's way too stimulating for me to even consider it. Other than that our sex life is fine and we have a good and loving relationship.

There are often major changes for the daughters sexually as sexuality issues get resolved.

> Until this week I would have checked this ["non-sexual"] as the answer to my own sexual identity. I've been asexual for the 10 years of my marriage but recently had a real breakthrough.

A CONFUSION OF SELVES: SEXUALITY AND GENDER IDENTITY

At the basis of the issues of sexuality, sexual orientation and gender identity for some daughters is the sexual confusion caused by and with the mothers. One survey section asked:

Q. Do you think your mother was ...	Yes	No	Unsure
Confused about her own sexual identity?	59%	17%	24%
Confused about your sexuality?	48%	16%	34%

Many of the respondents believe that their mothers had issues with their own sexual/gender identities. As reflected in the responses of the daughters on this survey, some mothers' issues involved bitterness about being female. This bitterness may have included resentments about the position or treatment of women in society, the focus on female sexuality (to the exclusion of other attributes such as intelligence, talent, empathy, and so on) by men, the lack of protection and support females receive, and abuse by women.

She HATED it!

She HATED being female.

Roughly half the daughters reported that their mothers were confused about their daughters' sexuality. This finding is significant because as young girls the daughters had to relate to their sexuality partly within the context of messages from their mothers.

She did not want me to be sexual. [The] abuse was related to the onset of my menstruation. [And] I do know she had an abortion when she was only 15.

This daughter's statement may reflect the common situation of some mothers projecting their unresolved pain onto their daughters.

Seventy-two percent (72%) of the daughters believe the abuse by their mothers caused their sexual confusion, and 52% of them said it probably caused them more sexual identity concerns than they might have had without the abuse. For example, when asked their current sexual status, 10% of the respondents to the survey reported they currently don't know or that they feel uncertain about their sexual identity. Forty-eight percent (48%) of the daughters reported childhood sexual identity issues, and this rose to 52% among the adult daughters.

To normalize in one's mind and within society's norms both same-sex relations and mother/daughter sex is, to say the least, challenging.

> Sexual identity? Currently don't know or feel uncertain and [am] trying to take a break — needing a period of celibacy. Sometimes afraid of the dark; cannot make love in the dark.

> Sexual identity problems ... it sometimes "blows my mind" that my mother felt like my first lover and I wonder how this impacts on [my] sexuality.

> I am definitely heterosexual, but I resent that I have to defend or "prove" it.

Some daughters feel a resistance to femininity and femaleness that may keep them from conforming to a typically female presentation of themselves to others. Some daughters wrote that they had difficult experiences determining their sexuality.

> It got me into the lunatic fringe of sadism and masochism, bondage, etc.

Voluntary and Involuntary Sexual Abstinence

Voluntary abstinence suggests a choice between real possibilities. Involuntary abstinence indicates that no other choice is possible, in this case because of the emotional and physical effects of sexual abuse. Fifteen percent of the daughters (15%) are currently nonsexual. Some of them feel sexually shut down and unable to be sexual with other people. Some daughters have concerns about re-experiencing traumatic sexual stimulation or over-stimulation. Others experience decreased interest in sex. Some daughters are sexually aroused only under certain circumstances.

> I feel uncertain. Perhaps the best description of me might be autosexual.

> [I'm] currently in a [long-term but unmarried relationship] but not sexual (4.5 years). Was sexual before my "grandmother memories."

> I have to manage the level of stimulation or my PTSD gets set off. At night I have to be able to lie still and awake for awhile to shutdown the day's impact. Until I can do that I have a hard time being able to take in sexual stimulation and respond. And I can't deal with sexual stimulation beyond the point of orgasm at all. It's too much and really overloads me in every way.

131

[I am] emotionally and sexually anorexic.

Outside my home [I] shut down unless using drugs or alcohol.

Heterosexuality

Forty-two percent (42%) of the daughters identify as heterosexual. Many of these daughters expressed social values that deem heterosexuality as "normal" sexuality and feel all sexuality should lead toward male/female sexual relations, marriage and family. These assumptions are a problem for some daughters because such a life appears to include becoming like their mothers. As a result, some daughters do not so much reject heterosexuality as feel reluctant to embrace it. As one daughter said, "*It's what she is.*"

[I'm] inclined towards heterosexuality.

Homosexuality

Thirty-six percent (36%) of the daughters in this study identified themselves as lesbians. At present, there are no clear reasons why humans become lesbians, homosexuals, bisexuals or heterosexuals. Developing a clear sexual orientation is a long, complex process. One theory is that people are born with a basic sexual orientation. "Choice" and "choosing" are perhaps invalid possibilities in discussing any sexual orientation. We can choose what we *do* with our sexuality.

I've often been asked if sexual abuse causes some daughters to become lesbians. The survey asked twice if the respondents felt the abuse caused them any difficulty with sexual identity issues. While 52% and 72% of the respondents said it did, it must be noted that "difficulty with sexual identity issues" is very different from a primary identification as a lesbian. I believe it is more accurate to say that sexual abuse by one's mother may force a more conscious formulation of adult sexuality than might have otherwise occurred, but that it does not "cause" lesbianism.

The number of lesbians in this sample is higher than the generally accepted estimate of 10% (based on Kinsey, 1953) of the general American population. After many conversations and contacts with survivors of sexual abuse by mothers, I believe that this incidence reflects the fact that a significant number of lesbians were more willing than heterosexuals to talk about a difficult sexual matter. Perhaps of all women, lesbians can tolerate talking about (or at least answering surveys about) being outside the female sexual "social norms" generally expected by this society. After all, they have dealt with homophobia both in their personal lives and in addressing the sexual abuse by their mothers.

On the other hand, being or even suspecting that they *may* be attracted to women is likely to be frightening and disturbing for some daughters of sexually abusive mothers because they may feel so strongly *"I don't want to be like her."* The homophobia we (including lesbians) are exposed to discourages some from seriously considering attraction to women — being lesbian or bisexual — so that these considerations may smolder for years.

> [I] had a hard time thinking it was okay for me to be a lesbian. I thought I should not be attracted to women.

There may not be freedom to explore these issues in adolescence, often the normal time for it, and exploration may have to wait for the safety of adulthood, after the abuse is over, or after all contact with the mother is ended. The result can range from total change to none. This exploration may be done without same-sex contact through honest self-examination.

For those who need to explore it, resolution can bring real relief.

> Sexually I was nothing until recently. I believe therapy has helped me, but more so, I believe that meeting a childhood friend who confessed herself to being an incest victim did much to help me. We became lovers — I for the first time at age 60.

The healthiest approach to establishing any sexual identity, in my view, is having the freedom to reach resolutions based on one's own needs and feelings. The survivor must sort out her sexual feelings and orientation for herself and separately from her mother.

> It [the abuse] has nothing to do with homosexuality.

Bisexuality

Ten percent (10%) of the daughters identified their sexual orientation as bisexual. An even larger number of the daughters may have had to consider attraction to both sexes to establish a clear and comfortable sexuality. Some have a true attraction to both men and women, and for others, it's a gnawing awareness that, as one female respondent put it, *"there's something between me and women."*

> [I think there needs to be research on] sexual identity — bisexualness. Does this relate to mother/daughter incest? Do we turn to other women because of our abuse?

Not everybody fit neatly into specific and unchanging sexual categories.

> But [I was] not aware of this [issue] until adulthood. [Now] I am committed to a monogamous heterosexual relationship, attracted to both genders, sometimes neither.

Internalized Homophobia

Homophobia is the fear and hatred of being homosexual or bisexual or of being so labeled. In the United States, it generally stems from strong core belief in gender-role stereotypes and fear of not measuring up to those images, or from religious beliefs that homosexuality is "immoral."

> A contributing factor to my desire to not reveal mother-daughter incest [in psychotherapy] was the homosexual implications. At the time I was extremely homophobic. This [was] by no means the total reason I didn't reveal it sooner, but it did contribute. The shame created by homophobia, both internally and societally. [This] must be dealt with prior to feeling okay relating this information.

Some daughters may have had or been aware of others' painful experiences with homophobia and social rejection. They may have been taught homophobia by their mother perpetrators as a part of the sexual abuse because their mothers feared their own sexuality.

Femininity and Gender Identity

A few respondents were uncomfortable being "female."

> I have always felt that I am, at least in part, male.

The connection for this daughter between internal feelings of being male and the fact that she was her mother's sexual object seem clear.

> I think there are very deep identity problems. In that it is difficult for me to connect with a healthy sense of being a woman. What is that? My role model as a child was so crazy and so much in denial about who she was that working on female issues (not just empowerment and feminist issues) but also on mothering, caring femininity [is difficult.] What is special about being a woman?

The following daughter, a successful professional, explains her ambivalence about being female.

> [I have] problems with femininity and identifying myself as a woman. Need to be perfectly groomed, extremely cultured, appear very feminine to keep away feelings of being an evil, disgusting hermaphrodite, stilted speech, and overly formal at times. Also need to be successful in a "male" occupation, have "male" outlook, strengths, opinions, abilities. Need to be titanically strong and powerful. Staying extremely thin to avoid being female, having a lot of disgusting female blubber, to minimize the body which got me into such trouble, to fast and atone my sins, to be clean and slight like a child — to the vanishing point. To distract myself with physical pain. I feel both male and female, having lived my life in a male power/achievement, ego state.

For these survivors, identity questions may or may not be about sexual orientation per se. For some daughters of sexually abusive mothers, identity considerations can be about not wanting to be like their abusers.

> I don't want to grow into a woman. I resent womanly functions and I never, NEVER want my body to look like my mother's.

> Am I male or female? Which sex do I relate to more?

Confusion about Sex and Love

Some daughters report confusion about sex and love. They often report a hunger for intimacy but may be either repelled by or compelled by sex.

> [I feel I have a] sexual addiction — confusing love/sex/nurturing.

REPEATING THE HARM

Many sex offender treatment providers have identified sexual abuse in the histories of their clients, suggesting that it may be a contributing factor (though never an exculpatory one) to their perpetrating behavior. In the conventional wisdom, this repetition is identified as the generational cycle of abuse: those who are abused may be more likely to become abusers and repeat the harm they have experienced.

Fear of Perpetrating Sexual Abuse

Although the survey did not ask directly, some of the daughters reported fear that as adults they might sexually abuse a child. Women are socialized to identify with their mothers and, for these women, that means identifying with a sexual abuse perpetrator. Many of the respondents also expressed concerns about abused children often becoming adult abusers.

> I never _did_ [abuse my children], but always worried that I might be inadvertently inappropriate when they were infants.

> I have had fears that I could [abuse a child] and have guarded against it.

Some daughters have carefully avoided contact with children or have opted to remain childless out of fear they might abuse.

> I avoid children. Is this neglect?

Clinically, these fears must always be taken seriously, while respecting the autonomy of the individual to make her own decisions about child rearing. However, I find it sad that child-rearing was an option foreclosed early and automatically for some daughters as a result of being abused by their mothers.

Actually the daughters in this sample report low levels of sexual abuse of children, with just 3% self-reporting that they had as adults abused a child. Somewhat more of the daughters (15%) reported that as children they had sexually abused other children, while 7% characterized some of their adult interactions with others as sexually abusive. Further research is needed to understand these self-reported low levels of perpetration more fully.

> I have also realized recently that although I didn't define the abuse myself, I have been afraid that I would be a child abuser. I tried all my life in many ways not to be like my mother and although I didn't consciously define the abuse, subconsciously I must have accepted it and was afraid that I would repeat it myself. Now that I have children of my own and have spent more time with children this fear has subsided. I know I will not be an abuser.

Some of the abusive behavior was experimental, and some constituted deliberate sexual aggression. Their self-reports of sexual abuse of children as adults is at a relatively low rate and seems to indicate that the women in this group worked hard to prevent themselves from offending, often by minimizing their exposure to vulnerable children. However, the level might be quite different among other groups of daughters, especially those with histories of other socially aggressive behaviors. Further research is needed to establish verified levels.

> All those abused do <u>not</u> become abusers!! (This idea fills me with more rage than anything else!!)

SEXUAL REVICTIMIZATION

This study suggests childhood revictimization of the daughters to be about 60% to 70% or higher. These numbers indicate that the daughters were four times more likely to be sexually abused by someone in addition to their mothers (60% of respondents) than to perpetrate a sexual offense against other children (15%). The adult daughters are often painfully aware of the impact of their mothers' sexual abuse against them.

> Since I remembered and discovered (now understand) that what happened to me was abuse I have remembered 3 men who sexually abused me as a child (earliest memory was 4 years old). I believe that the inappropriateness of my mother from birth set me up to be an incest victim throughout my childhood.

> The memories are just now coming back. Mother may have been part of a cult. When [my] mother stopped, neighbors and my brother started. They used me by selling me to old men. [It] lasted in varying degrees to age 12. She made me unable to be loved normally by anyone ever again.

The following account of one daughter's revictimization is one of the more extreme and demonstrates the continuing vulnerability created by early abuse.

> When I was 3 to 5 a male neighbor (approximately 25 to 30 years old) took me for a walk to a secluded spot. He wanted me to touch his penis and offered me an orange lollipop in exchange for licking it.
>
> When I was 4 or 5 years old an uncle who lived with us forced me to have anal intercourse with him. He had a gun and threatened to kill me if I wasn't quiet or if I told.
>
> When I was about six I think I was involved in abuse by one of my grandfathers.
>
> At about age 9 to 11 there was at least 2 or 3 incidents of sexual abuse. A stranger made me have oral sex with him at a park inside a building where the showers were. This was something I experienced as if a witness across the room. My brother had been nearby or actually witnessed the incident

and I was taken home by the police. (I'm not sure they knew the extent of what had taken place.) My father beat me after this incident. The abuse and the beating were a sort of "last straw" for me. I told myself I had to face the fact that my parents didn't love me. Around this time I began a years-long period of preoccupation with suicide.

I was abused by my brother who is 6 years older than me and when I was 17 I was molested by a 39-year-old male teacher.

Another daughter raises the topic of prevention and how it might have been different for these daughters as little girls.

The [Say] No, Go [Somewhere Safe], and Tell [Someone who will help you] stuff [programs designed to teach children to be safe] are not going to reach [the child victims of sexual abuse by mothers]. If you can't tell your mother how the hell can you tell anyone [else]?

Too many prevention programs assume a protective and non-abusive mother.

Sixty-two percent of the respondents (62%) report that they were sexually revictimized as adults. This level is appallingly high. According to their self-reports they are twenty times more likely to be sexually revictimized as adults than to sexually abuse a child. These daughters have been raped, some more than once, by strangers, and/or they were in abusive relationships and marriages. They have been sexually victimized by professionals they have gone to for help, including therapists and medical professionals. Many believe the abuse by their mothers set them on a path of tolerance of abuse.

[I had] several lesbian relationships which were emotionally and sexually abusive.

LONG-TERM PROBLEMS RELATED TO ASSOCIATED PHYSICAL ABUSE

The daughters who experienced *physical* abuse by their mothers were asked to assess whether that abuse had an impact on their adult sexual lives. Sixty percent (60%) said it did; 13% said it did not; and 18% of these incest victims were unsure. The daughters who experienced physical abuse may fear similar abuse by adult sex partners.

Sexual abuse by a woman can lead to very confused feelings regarding your OWN sexuality. [And] if sexual abuse was closely associated with physical abuse the client may become sexually aroused to real or fantasied stimuli dealing with the physical pain (e.g. being spanked).

Their abusive experiences may interfere with the freedom to be sexual and use their bodies to express and receive love and intimacy.

CHAPTER 10

The Pain Within:
Other Abuse-Related Issues

Daughters of sexually abusive mothers encounter or develop a number of psychological and emotional issues beyond those discussed so far, according to the survey responses. Some issues they share with survivors of male abusers, while others reflect the unique twist that comes from having been abused by mother, the person most like you in gender, the most influential, powerful person in a child's life.

BODY BETRAYAL

The daughters often have body distortions or a sense of being betrayed by their own bodies. They may dislike any physical features they share with their mothers' bodies. They may also dislike any aspects of her that they or others see in themselves, such as manner, voice, or laugh. They may feel their bodies have betrayed them by linking them to their perpetrators or that their bodies are flawed or can't be trusted. They may feel they are housed in bodies that symbolize the abuse.

> Being terrified of getting pregnant — psychic infertility. MY WOMB WAS STOLEN!

Add to these feelings a sense of sexual identity or gender confusion or the craving of food, alcohol, or drugs for numbing purposes, and the body becomes a mistrusted entity.

Body Image

Many daughters responding to the survey report being uncomfortable with their bodies, especially with physical features they feel resemble their mothers. These features range from the entire body, face, or to isolated features such as the knuckles or feet. The following statement illustrates the problem and its probable cause.

> The actual time span of the abuse was intermittent, a couple of months when I was very young, and later two discrete episodes (days); one when I was 5 and one at 6 years old. But the sense of revulsion toward her touch or seeing her naked has stayed with me and has flared up repeatedly throughout childhood and adulthood — also [I feel] a sense of revulsion towards my own body for ways it resembles hers.

Formerly abused daughters are often uncomfortable looking, sounding, breathing or smelling like their mothers. They may feel a deep and uncomfortable connection between their mothers and their own femininity, starting at very young ages.

> My mother had a venereal disease and I am often afraid I am dirty and unclean myself.

Likewise, the daughters are often sensitive to even casual comments pointing out similarities with their mothers. One woman I know has asthma and is very uncomfortable with her breathing during asthma attacks because it sounds like her aging mother's labored breaths.

Sexual Abuse Turned In On the Self

Some daughters become punitive with their bodies in a sexual manner.

[I'm] sexually abusive to myself — engaging in painful sex — particularly after a new memory or re-experiencing a feeling.

Adult Sexual Acting Out

Several daughters reported experiences like the following:

[I believe I had a] sexual addiction. At one time to cope with my pain I had several sexual partners. I was married, plus I had my female lover living with my husband and I, and I had other lesbian relationships outside the home.

NUMBING THE PAIN: SUBSTANCE ABUSE PATTERNS

Not surprisingly, especially given the generational and possible genetic or biological influence of the mothers and "other parents," the daughters reported relatively high rates of substance abuse, with the substance of choice being primarily — but not exclusively — alcohol. Usually this behavior is clinically interpreted as self-medication from the psychic pain of abuse, though generational role-modeling factors and self-destructive motivations should not be ignored.

Thirty-eight percent (38%) of respondents reported they had engaged in substance abuse in childhood, and 44% reported the incidence of such abuse in adulthood.

Using the APA's rates (from a 1980–85 community study based on *DSM III* criteria) as a gauge, it appears that *during childhood, the survivor daughters already had substance abuse problems at a rate three times the national adult average* (APA, 1994, p. 202 for alcohol rates, for example). In the context of our current drug and alcohol abuse epidemic, we must ask if we are addressing the real problems or the symptoms; that is, what psychic or emotional pain are children taking drugs to medicate?

The earliest reported alcohol abuse in this study was by the following respondent.

[I did] early alcohol abuse [at] five years of age.

This daughter's mother died of cirrhosis. These daughters too often learned to self-medicate their pain when left to their own devices with limited social support. Their parents were often their prime role model for this behavior.

The next daughter's statement explicitly links her sexual abuse experiences and her adult substance abuse tendencies:

> I have increased my alcohol intake in the past year when dealing with [the abuse].

At least one daughter related to cigarettes in terms of substance abuse and addiction and shared her struggle with the most common numbing drug.

> At age 38 I quit smoking after 25 years. Smoking to me was like alcohol to an alcoholic. I just lost it emotionally. I was crying all the time and depressed and thinking long thoughts on death. I got back into therapy with a woman who is into adult children of alcoholic issues.

Food and Eating Disorders

For some daughters, their abusable substance of choice was or is food. Asked about their own food consumption, the daughters reported childhood eating disorders (62%) and adult eating disorders (63%). In addition, 61% of the respondents reported adult weight problems (more than 20% above or 10% below ideal weight).

In the general population, 1% of girls between 12 and 18 years of age have anorexia nervosa, and perhaps as many as 5% of female college students may have bulimia (Nelson, Behrman, & Kliegman, 1990, pp. 67–69). Compared to these data, the rate of childhood eating disorders was very high among the respondent daughters. They may be reporting primarily on weight problems, but there may also be a significant incidence of anorexia and bulimia among the societally reinforced female dissatisfactions with body size and shape. Several respondents mentioned compulsive dieting. Weight was an emotionally volatile question for some daughters.

> This is an oppressive question! "Ideal weight" is a cultural norm created by white male, middle class, WASP doctors. The eating disorders question should be sufficient without asking about weight.

Food and mothers are so intertwined for the daughters that it's hard to separate them. Food is used for discipline, rewards, emotional expression, cultural pride, and many other things. For the child it is also the fuel used to achieve a size greater than or equal to the mother's; it can hide the body, self-soothe hurt feelings, express anger, or can even be used as an instrument of rejection by refusing the mother's food. The roots of many eating problems are established in childhood and can lead to life-long struggles. One reports: *"[I still either] go overboard or don't eat for days."*

In this culture, body weight is tied to self-image, self-esteem, body image, and often social acceptance. In addition, a survivor abused by her mother is faced with conscious or unconscious feelings about looking like her mother, being her size, or never wanting to be "her size." There is a temptation to feel stronger and more powerful than the mother by growing larger, to avoid feeling vulnerable if smaller than the mother. Some daughters feel a need to be larger than the size they were when they were abused. Some daughters may suddenly feel vulnerable if they diet down to the weight they were when they were abused.

> When I was a slightly overweight teen, I was told by an acquaintance of my family that, if I kept gaining weight, I would be "Bigger than my mother." That has stuck with me and has made me NEED to be large for protection. I feel mentally ready to give that up, but have a lot of fear about losing strength.

Some daughters have used weight as a weapon, a way to thwart their mothers' wishes regarding body size, especially when mothers had focused on the daughters' bodies.

> FOOD — [my] weapon against her. The fat was mine.

This daughter reports that her adult self-mutilation and silent expression of rage at her mother resulted in a weight in excess of 600 pounds.

Weight manipulation can be motivated by the desire for food and nurture from one's mother or reflect rejection of her food and her nurture. Such manipulation may reflect a desire to hide or flaunt sexuality, and may indicate anger at doctors who did not protect the daughters when protection was needed, or anger at any doctor who now wants to protect the survivor's health.

A daughter's eating and weight problems may address food or the lack of it, food withheld as punishment, or fleeing childhood poverty; food may be the numbing drug of choice. Eating disorders may be an attempted mechanism of self-nurture or self-punishment gone terribly awry. Eating disorders may be the haunting effects of child neglect or chronic depression that can cause long-term lethargy and resulting weight gain.

I think back now and I believe my weight issues are partly to put something between me and the sexual anxiety I felt from my mother and also that I identified with my father since he made the most sense to me between the two of them. So I ate like him and one of the few things I look back on in my childhood with much pleasure is that my mother cooked well. It was in some ways the most consistent pleasure I received from her. Years later my father confirmed that she would not allow me to eat sometimes even though I had to sit at the table while others did. He said she'd slap me if I touched her or tried to get food. I was in a high chair during some of it.

Problems with food seem to emerge quite early. Some report emotional problems with food and weight starting before age five.

In my work with survivors of sexual abuse by mothers, I've met over 25 women whose weight is in the 300- to 600-pound range. They often tell me that their mothers showed great concern and caring about their weight and that as children they were frequently taken to doctors for their problems. For some, the weight can't come off until issues with their mothers are resolved.

Some of the mothers demanded absolute control over their children's food intake. A few daughters report near-starvation during early childhood. Whatever the cause of adult weight problems resulting from mother/daughter abuse, they seem to be often formed well before the latency years.

I was often literally called "One More Mouth To Feed" because I was the youngest child. There were dinner table discussions involving my entire family about if I should be allowed to eat. These were like mock trials regarding my worthiness to eat. And everyone got a voice in those decisions except me. My current behaviors, the look on my face at the moment, how much I weighed were often the major focuses and how I reacted to these discussions was used as a measure of "if I was really hungry" at any given meal.

This often went on until my older siblings were eating second helpings of food which I was afraid would disappear. If I cried I was called a "cry baby." If I got visibly angry (which I often did) I was punished by the withholding of food and being sent from the table without eating or completing a meal. Desert was always contingent on my behavior. The ironic thing is my mother was a good cook so I felt doubly frustrated.

As a result of all this I learned to eat fast and still do. I learned very young to eat what I could find outdoors and regularly stole from gardens and neighbor's fruit trees and bushes. I learned to love potlucks. I got a job at age ten cleaning for an old lady every week mostly because she'd feed me lunch as part of my benefit package. I graduated from there to restaurants where I could also eat. From junior high school on I managed to buy a school hot lunch ticket every week. Other kids would complain about the food but I loved it and that ticket was like freedom for me. Today I seldom leave my house without money for a meal in my pocket.

When she was really uptight she would go after my body with hair pulling, lots of slapping, physical threats, and sometimes what would have to be called beatings. During those periods there was constant manipulation with food. This ranged from serving me four or five times what anyone would consider a normal serving of oatmeal which I had to eat before I could leave the table, to withholding food for a day or two and then strictly controlling what I could eat. I think getting control of food, comforting myself with it, and the abuse are all tied together.

Issues with food are slowly getting better for me but I know they are very connected to my abuse as a child and to my mother and my need for nurture. But it's still an emotional area and I'm aware that as I think and write about this my impulse is to eat something.

The questions about food in this study merely scratched the surface of this aspect of sexual abuse by mothers, and more research is needed.

CHAPTER 11

Effects on the Mind and Heart:
Mental Health

<hr>

Poor mental health is easier to identify than good mental health. Major elements of good mental health are defined here as: a) the ability to stay in the "here and now"; b) awareness of and coping with emotions and thoughts; c) a good orientation to present reality; d) being reasonably unblocked in the ability to be productive and active in life; and e) the absence of mental and emotional illness. Clinicians widely accept the theory that unresolved childhood trauma significantly disrupts good mental health.

LOST CHILDHOODS: DEVELOPMENTAL DISRUPTION DUE TO SEXUAL ABUSE

When the daughters were asked if they felt they were ever "a child in the true sense of the word," 16% of the women answered yes, 72% said no, and 12% of them answered that they were unsure. Many feel they were not allowed to have a "normal" childhood, though some daughters remember bits and pieces of comfort in childhood.

It was absolutely forbidden.

[I had it] when I lived with my grandmother from ages 3 to 5 or 6.

The daughters often had childhoods cut short by years. During their adulthood, many may need support and permission to grieve for lost childhoods and encouragement to enjoy life with at least moments of child-like safety and privilege.

Play saved me as a child. The comraderie and laughter of fun in playing meant so much.

Fifty-three percent (53%) of the daughters felt overwhelmed during childhood, a percentage that increased to 65% of the respondents in adulthood. They often remember very little of their childhoods with pleasure. The overwhelming feelings often lead to what may be described as feeling "frozen."

In this section, we explore the daughters' developmental process, childhood responses to the sexual abuse, and some adult outcomes. To help in understanding these processes and responses, I have classified the daughters' problems in the following categories: 1) failure to bond and remaining un-bonded; 2) fusion with mothers; 3) exploding into premature independence; 4) social and emotional failure to thrive; and 5) difficulty becoming separate individuals.

The Abandoned: The Failure to Bond

Some theorists believe that bonding with the mother should occur soon after the child is born; if it doesn't, the infant may not grow or thrive properly. Children whose skin and body are not touched often become socially withdrawn and apathetic by their second year of life. Severe lack of bonding leads to physical failure to thrive and, in the worst cases, to a child's death.

At very early ages, it may be nearly impossible for a daughter to withdraw from an abusive mother. To leave even the appearance of protection by the mother may cause them to face dangers similar to those of a young stray animal. Many in this study could identify with the feeling of being a "stray child."

> There is a different quality to being abused by a mother as opposed to being sexually abused by anyone else. This is difficult to explain. It may have to do with the devastation and betrayal of the mother-child bond.

> There was emotional abuse and neglect throughout my childhood. I was raped in the second grade and my mother never even noticed! I took care of it myself.

However, the alternative to being a "stray child" may be to risk even greater fusion with the mother, including continual struggles over boundaries and submission. To seek information about the need for bonding and independence, the survey asked questions about physical, emotional and behavioral aspects of their relationships with their mothers.

A Merged Child: Fusion with an Abusive Mother

One daughter wrote the following about her sexually abusive mother:

> I was not a separate person to her. In her mind we were fused.

In these cases, fusion means the experience of mothers continuing to engage emotionally with their daughters until the emotional boundaries between them may be profoundly blurred. This fusion is always at the expense of the child.

> It [the sexual abuse], for me, was part of an overall relationship in which I was allowed no boundaries or identity. I feel like she sucked my brains out with a soda straw so she could fill me with her own identity.

Feeling forced to choose between identity-crushing submission or abandonment is an appalling dilemma. If the daughter submits, she may find her life overwhelmed by her mother's, and this makes thinking about the mother's eventual death stressful.

I used to worry about this <u>all the time</u> and her death <u>was</u> extremely traumatic for me. I never made the connection — it's fusion!

For some daughters of abusing mothers, it's difficult to verbalize this fusing or merging of personae.

My therapist has been very gently pointing out areas of enmeshment between my mother and I. I just thought of my mother as "over protective and overly motherly." I have a friend who is an incest survivor and when she would talk about her father I would wonder why I had some of those same feelings about my mother. Now, through a series of events, my mother came to live with me temporarily. She's leaving soon for a retirement village!

My partner of 8 years began to see some of my mother's crazy thinking and crazy logic. That made me feel wonderful. I would say "Yes. That's what I grew up with. That's what I grew up with. That's what I've been trying to tell you!"

Children are normally enmeshed with their mothers at very young ages. At infancy, a child may not be able to tell where his or her mouth leaves off and the mother's breast begins. Slowly, a process of separation occurs, and children become separate individuals; however, in cases of mother/daughter fusion due to sexual and other abuse, the child is often not allowed even to learn where she leaves off and her mother begins.

To be so enmeshed with one's perpetrator can be devastating. If we think of sexual bonding rather than parent/child bonding, we can see that the entire development of the child is altered dramatically. In abusive relationships, the focus of the entire relationship may be the mother's needs, including sexual ones, rather than the child's growth.

It's unclear to me how much of the merging between my mother and me was actually sexual abuse. It's difficult to separate what was affection and what was sexual.

In some respondents' relationships, some of the mothers' personae also merged with the daughters.'

To grow up, to become independent, to achieve a sense of self requires the development of psychological boundaries. When your body is the <u>possession</u> of your mother, for her gratification, you have great difficulty understanding where you end and the other person begins, which makes it hard to function in <u>any</u> capacity.

It [the abuse by mother] creates specific "boundary" problems — absolute internalization and identification with abuser so that victim/survivor can't find her own "self" separate from mother.

This lack of boundaries and support for separation and growth can lead to problems in other relationships for the abused daughters.

> I chose a male survivor of incest with his mother for an 11-year relationship, repeating a lot of the patterns with my mother all over again — including sexual abuse on both sides. Needless to say, I identified so much with him, even (especially?) in my denial of my own incest, that we merged. He never got into recovery for his incest, and I only acknowledged my own incest immediately after I left the relationship.

> [I have] difficult relationships with other women.

MOTHER INTROJECTS AS A FORM OF FUSION

Introjection is a complex psychological process that occurs when a person adopts some or all aspects of someone else, which then become a part of the person. Everyone naturally experiences this to some degree with parents. When healthy aspects are incorporated, they can serve as a supportive infrastructure to an emerging personality. This incorporating of personal traits, values, or beliefs can function like the studs or beams buried in the walls of a house; it gives us support long after we forget its presence. However, when the introjected qualities are negative, and, for example, a daughter assimilates many traits of an unhealthy mother, it can create intense and potentially damaging inner strife.

Many daughters possess aspects of their mothers' personalities, physical appearance, or interests. Some sexually abused daughters, however, may feel that their mothers have poisoned their potential to become healthy women. They may feel that parts of their mothers now live within them. Just as the daughters may come to loathe and mistrust their mothers, they may come to loathe and mistrust anything in themselves that they believe comes from their mothers. These feelings can be profoundly disturbing. A daughter may feel that just as her mother was abusive to her from outside, the mother can now be abusive and destructive from inside the daughter as well.

Small children cannot articulate these feelings, but looking back as adults, the daughters may not only see the destructiveness of their mothers, but "feel" it still exists within them. In the following detailed statement, it appears the daughter is or has been deeply fragmented as a person or personality. She explains how involved her introjected mother was in that fragmentation, and begins by telling how her mother "lives" within her:

153

> There's a woman who lives inside my body/mind who is NOT part of the comprehensive/entity called K_____ (the name by which I'm called, my birth name.) This woman who shares [my] body bears my mother's name.

She next explains how the introjection occurred and still functions, and how fragmentation helps her cope with her old pain.

> Intellectually I understand that this woman in me is an introject of the "bad mother." I perceived my mother as good and bad, but couldn't tolerate perceiving her as bad, and so she — the bad mother — became a part of me, while the mother that "I" (another part of me) remembered is the good mother. However, other parts of me have preserved — for better or worse — memories of my mother behaving in ways no one would consider good. These memories began leaking through to "I" when I was 32.

This description depicts a complex relationship among the various "splits" or parts of this daughter. Some parts have managed to view the mother as good despite a conflicting reality of bad experiences known by other parts within her. She goes on to explain the conflicts she experiences with her introjected mother. This internalized mother is a strong and vividly felt inner force.

> This introjects stuff is powerful and therapists need to understand it. My particular brand of maternal introject despises me, except, "NO," she says, "I love my children. I am the perfect 'good enough mother.' If you think I hate you, it's because you're crazy." But then she turns around again and tells me I deserve to be smeared into the ground like dog shit. She threatens to kill me (and I believe she has the power to do so), and then denies having done so. She [the bad mother] doesn't interact with anyone other than me — with the exception of a couple of occasions when she's talked with my therapist.
>
> I experience this introject as more than tapes that play in my head (i.e., the scripts we all bear from childhood). I _feel_ her presence in me. When she assaults me, I simultaneously feel her feelings and my own. For an instant, when she is despising me, I feel waves of despising/hating going through my body and I feel myself to be despicable. _And_ I feel emotionally/kinesthetically as if I'm being despised/hated.
>
> Another example is when I feel in my body her cackling, cruel, desire/thrust/drive to humiliate me, I also feel myself to be ridiculous, obscene, revolting _and_ I feel emotionally/kinesthetically as if I'm being humiliated, cackled at, sneered at. Much — well, some, at least — of my day-to-day experience of living is a response to the maternal introject.

Imagine the energy it would take to control the impact of this introjected mother/force. Given this internal struggle, imagine how she might sometimes appear to an outside observer from whom the conflict is hidden.

Professional helpers must understand how fundamentally these introjects can be experienced. This introjection is like living at very close quarters with the most internalized critical, and perhaps mentally ill, parent.

NO PRIVACY, NO SELF: BOUNDARIES OVERWHELMED

Sexual offenses by mothers are often different from those by other offenders because in their role as chief caretaker, mothers have unlimited and socially supported access to their victims. In this circumstance, a mother can often overwhelm any boundaries the daughter tries to establish, especially during the child's early years.

> To grow up, to become independent, to achieve a sense of self requires the development of psychological boundaries. When your body is the POSSESSION of your mother, for her gratification, you have great difficulty understanding where you end and the other person begins, which makes it hard to function in ANY capacity.

Boundary violation is often a critical issue for the daughters.

> This is a very important issue to me. To quote from The Courage To Heal: "Since children frequently bond most closely with their mothers, abuse by mothers in particular, can leave a child with severe lack of boundaries between herself and her offender" (page 97). That expresses my own experience so well.

The following respondent comments on the reasons for understanding this issue fully. Read her words while remembering that the average age the abuse started in this study was 3.2 years old.

> The boundary issues with which a woman who has been sexually abused by her mother struggles are enormous. It may be that a lot could be learned (a lot more than is known now) about the formation of ego boundaries in "normal" circumstances from studying the boundary difficulties of those of us raised in this abnormal circumstance. When, as in my case, the abuse begins in infancy, boundaries are even more nebulous things.

The absence of boundaries may come to feel normal and lead to long-term complications. This important issue must be discussed in therapy, with good boundaries demonstrated by all therapists.

Growing Up Too Soon: Exploding Into Premature Independence

Common responses to enmeshment with abusive mothers can range from prolonging childhood and dependency to compression and obliteration of it. This range is roughly illustrated on the chart below.

RANGE OF DAUGHTERS' REACTIONS TO MATERNAL SEXUAL ABUSE

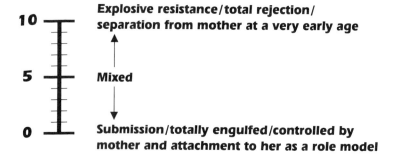

10 — **Explosive resistance/total rejection/ separation from mother at a very early age**

5 — **Mixed**

0 — **Submission/totally engulfed/controlled by mother and attachment to her as a role model**

Survivors whose reactions are at the more submissive end of such a scale may feel overwhelmed and unprepared to face life. They may feel they do not know how to create security for themselves. Those who resist fusion with their mothers may have to do it in such powerful and forceful ways that they find themselves emotionally and/or physically expelled from the family circle before they are prepared to manage their lives. These daughters may instinctively mistrust intimacy or become fiercely independent very early in life. However, as children outside the family, they will undoubtedly face new difficulties and dangers.

The daughters may be forced to make dramatic and powerful decisions about how to cope while maintaining virtual silence about the cause of their distress. They may be too young to articulate why they are behaving as they do, yet feel forced to do so. Conscious or not, the daughters shift away from normal childhood developmental processes and into defensive and distorted ones.

Those who avoid fusion through compression or a shortening of their childhoods are often fleeing to adulthood and away from their mothers. Initially, they may feel relief at escape, but later they may feel they lost their childhoods too early.

An abusive mother may have unlimited access to a daughter and can sap the child's energies to the point where the child does not establish a self separate from the abusive mother. Until the daughter separates sufficiently and has control over her own energy, she cannot nurture and strengthen herself. The mother may continue to see the child as a tool for her own gratification with no recognition of the child as separate or valued in her own right. If these unseparated daughters experience rejection by their mothers, they may expend their energies attempting to recreate the fusion in order to have a sense of self because that's what they experience as normal.

The daughters may feel developmentally incongruent or abnormal for their ages. When they become grown women, they may feel immature and vulnerable when in contact with their mothers. Continued sexual activity or even memories of past abuse threaten an emotional re-enmeshment and drain on their psychological energies. Many experience their mothers as emotional flypaper: the mother is a sticky, difficult presence or memory who maintains the power to make the daughter feel "stuck" again.

Many daughters attempted to become independent at very early ages, turning away from the mother in nearly every way.

Independent!! Absolutely rejecting of her!!

[I was] falsely mature.

When the daughters became independent at early ages, such autonomy may have backfired on them; they were then expected to be even more independent, or it was forced upon them rather than chosen.

My mother has told me that she didn't know how to relate to anyone who didn't need her and by 3 years old I was [in her words] "independent and didn't need" her!

The daughters often burst into a pseudo-independence at ages far younger than child development theories predict, but such independence was not always easy.

> [I did] mothering of others as a way of nurturing myself. Sometimes good and sometimes bad.

This early independence is often so remarkably total and fierce that it later blocks the daughters from receiving help and support in even the smallest ways. It's a "Little Red Hen" method of growing up in which the daughter mostly raises herself because experience teaches her that others cannot be trusted.

FREEDOM FEARED AND DESIRED: DEPENDENCE VS. INDEPENDENCE

All children are dependent and need a constant caretaker. However, sexually abused daughters may develop mixed feelings about being dependent upon their abusive mothers, and these concerns are sometimes generalized to other relationships.

Eighty-five percent (85%) of the 93 daughters reported feelings of dependency in adulthood along with frequent deep mistrust of being dependent on anyone.

> [I have a] fear of dependency on others. [I] fear needing people and fear abandonment, or of feeling helpless, powerless, or trapped with no way out.

Such ambivalence can become a core issue for the daughters and linger for years even in trusted, loving adult relationships. Early "pseudo-independence" and extreme independence may be a defense against feeling even normal dependency.

Some daughters may feel like an empty hole needing to be filled by others. They may have one or more "inner children" desperate for their mothers' love. Some are stuck in wanting their mothers to "love them out of their empty feelings." Or they look for a substitute "good mother" to fill that hole in them. At the same time, these daughters are often remarkably independent, functional adults in other areas of their lives. This independence is a case of missing affiliations or bonds more than an overall breakdown of personal growth.

Seventy percent (70%) of the respondents report being aware of dependency related to the abuse as adults. They may try hard to present a brave and independent face, but inside they may feel secretly dependent.

> I grew into who I could be after I left home. I am very independent — but I have always had certain dependency issues.

Many daughters cannot or simply refuse to use their mothers as models. The problem with this approach to independence is that there may be no clear replacement model for such a daughter if she deliberately chooses not to emulate her mother, possibly leading to identity confusion.

These daughters had a homosexual experience in a homophobic society with someone the rest of society prefers to see as non-sexual. Their sexual secret runs head on into the homophobia and causes a major dilemma. Adolescent confusion and emotionalism may make it difficult to resolve this dilemma early in life. This dilemma may be compounded by a daughter's increasing similarity to her mother as time passes, if not in the exact physical features, then in adult female shape and size.

Social and Emotional Failure to Thrive

A CHILD FORSAKEN: ABANDONMENT VS. ATTACHMENT

These children are abandoned by their mothers through sexual behavior and by their fathers by their failure to protect. These children may also deny their own emotional needs for nurturance and place a higher priority on the need to escape the abuse or pursue early independence. Their young pseudo-adult state is really a form of self-abandonment because they must leave their childhood needs and young selves behind. Later, they are often ashamed and fearful of emotionally needy parts of themselves; the daughters fear further abandonment because they cannot always maintain an integrated adult self.

> I get it that there's a child in me but I don't know if I can stand her when she [cries] about her mommy.

Abandonment issues are often connected with these women's fathers also, as one survivor noted:

> I have major issues with men because my father abandoned me and I was sexually abused by other males, including doctors.

159

> Sexual abuse by your mother is a very frightening issue for the client to address in therapy. If they face their own experience they face the fact that they never really had that dreamy, idealized safety net called "Mom." They have to face very starkly that experience never existed for them. It may have only been fantasies or aggrandized/ overblown ideas or memories for other people also but they still have the option to cling to that image that their mom loved them.

> But we have to face the fact that it just wasn't there for us. Maybe never was. At least not in a way that we could take in and absorb. I suspect that for human beings there are fewer or deeper psychological bottom-line pits than for the "kid" in us to face that our mothers were there but either they didn't really love us or didn't care what happened to us. Especially given what society says is supposed to be true.

Through any failure to bond, the seeds of self-loathing are planted, and the survivor may come to believe, no matter how unconsciously, that if she admits her normal needs for human connections and acceptance, she is flawed as a person. These seeds can flourish in the fertile ground of low self-esteem and self-doubt. The daughters often feel that, "If my Mom doesn't love me, then who really does and what good am I?" These seeds may grow into monster weeds of horrible proportions.

Children (and adults) find it extremely painful to wonder whether their mothers never loved and wanted them. To open that door leads to questions such as, "Why did she have me?" Forty-four percent (44%) of the respondents state that their relationship with their mother was never healthy or never functioned well. Many have come to feel they were never "mothered."

Perhaps among the most telling pieces of data in the survey is the finding that 84% of the daughters report feeling that they became "stuck" at an early developmental stage, and roughly one third report feeling they were emotionally fragmented or "split" as a personality at one year of age or younger. These data indicate that early bonding was problematic for many of these mothers and daughters.

LEFT ALONE OR LONELY:
FEAR OF INTIMACY VS. DESIRE FOR INTIMACY

Eighty-three percent (83%) of the adult daughters reported difficulty with intimacy and this too likely has its roots in their childhood abuse.

> [I went into treatment because I was] wanting to have an intimate relationship and finding myself unable to.

Intimacy can be frightening for some daughters.

[This was true] before I met my husband. [I'd like to know more about the] history of relationships [for survivors of mother/daughter abuse] — healthy and unhealthy.

A MOTHER'S BETRAYAL:
MISTRUST VS. TRUST

Daughters' questioning of their mothers' trustworthiness may apply not only to other individuals or people in general, but to their security in life. For example, in answer to questions about confidence in their security, the following data show a pattern of erosion of daughters' feelings of security during childhood and later consequences:

Childhood anxiety	73%
Childhood fears related to the sexual abuse	84%
Adult trust problems	90%

Many daughters believe the abuse caused major, long-lasting trust difficulties.

Trust is very, very hard.

It creates a situation where there's absolutely no one to be trusted. No one to trust.

(I had) difficulty trusting at any level.

I think the distinction you made [during a training] about the bond between mother and child is very important. In a nutshell, if you can't trust your mother, who[m] can you trust? It is different from other violations.

It's a deeper wound than other sexual abuse. The betrayal and destruction of trust is so profound there are really no words to describe it.

It does happen. The victim never gets over it. The "ultimate trust of a child" is broken forever. A substitute "good" role model (in my case grandparents) can be very nurturing and help set "goals and patterns" for the child.

Continued contact with mothers may create even more mistrust, as one daughter reports:

> As one of my sisters put it, "It's impossible to tell where the sickness ends and the evil begins." We try to be charitable and think of her as mentally ill, but she's so damn malicious!

Fearful children have difficulties deciding whom they can trust, and this may make staying with baby-sitters, starting school, or even playing with other children frightening.

Only 20 percent of the daughters indicated that they had a very involved social life outside their families. Some daughters had almost no home life and little or no emotional commitment to their biological relatives. Their alternative social connections may or may not have been healthy influences. The secrets and pain drive many away from their homes and families. Any concerns they have regarding sexuality may cause them to feel vulnerable in new ways. They may flee to others who, they believe, are less faultfinding and/or homophobic.

TOO YOUNG FOR HER AGE: SOCIAL IMMATURITY

Forty-four percent (44%) of the daughters reported a sense of childhood immaturity, which they believe was connected to their abuse. This type of immaturity tends to show in clinginess, shyness, a lack of social skills, emotional and social underdevelopment, and a general naïveté. This immaturity may result from the above pattern of social withdrawal as a coping mechanism.

DIFFICULTY BECOMING SEPARATE INDIVIDUALS

Every human must struggle to become an established, adult individual. The path is sometimes unclear and dangerous, and the climb is not always encouraged or supported.

Sexual abuse by mothers occurs in a relationship which is deeply entwined with other experiences such as child care, nourishment, learning, socialization, sex role modeling, and development of parenting skills. Once the bond becomes sexualized, the children find it very difficult to disengage the self. The abuse often begins when children are developmentally most focused on their mothers. Such abuse leaves a survivor with a need to understand the abnormal in order to make sense out of their own experiences.

As some daughters look back, they are profoundly aware of how deeply affected they have been by the destructive and abusive relationships they experienced. They wonder what life would have been like with different parents, with more protection and support. Many simply persevere.

My whole life is different than it would have been if she had been O.K. Every single choice I made was influenced by her actions.

❏

But no thanks to her. I have done it myself.

❏

How would I know who I could be other than who I am?

❏

I developed differently than I would have.

ESTABLISHING INDEPENDENT RELATIONSHIPS

Fifty-six percent (56%) said they have been able to establish independent relationships with others but 20% of respondents say they have not. Many feel they have difficulty achieving independent and balanced relationships.

Equal friendships…yes. Sexually intimate relationships…no. Almost every relationship carries sexual fear.

Many daughters develop an early tendency to socially withdraw, and this often continues throughout their lives. When asked about it, they reported as follows:

Childhood restricted social life	**57%**
Childhood withdrawal	**74%**
Adult feeling isolated	**85%**
Adult social isolation	**59%**

I felt total isolation from "normal" people.

Many learn to avoid contact with others.

[I was] very shy with other people, very timid about life, with vague fears that something terrible would happen if I tried any experience away from my family; (e.g., going to the neighbors to play, going on a field trip at school).

[I would] go into a closet with a flashlight and a book and stay there for the day.

[I became] very withdrawn and anti-social.

THE HURT THAT CAN'T BE SEEN: IMPACT OF TRAUMA ON MENTAL HEALTH

Traumas are events that cause distress and interfere with good mental health. The severity and frequency of exposure to the traumatic stressors determine the severity of their impact. Whether the traumas were accidental, random, or deliberate makes a difference as well. The impact of unresolved traumas is clear. For example, individuals who survived the Nazi concentration camps developed a common set of symptoms called KZ syndrome which included sleep disturbances, memory problems, anxiety and chronic dysphoria, and gastrointestinal problems (Usdin & Lewis, 1979, p. 205).

There are two important points to make which will help us to understand the effects of the trauma suffered by the daughters in this study.

First, in traumatic situations such as war, airplane crashes, and earthquakes, the survivors know that "normal" circumstances will exist even if rescue or the return of "normal" circumstances was delayed. The belief that things can improve or safety will be restored is important. With restabilization or a return to "normal" circumstances, stress and symptoms such as disturbed sleep usually decrease. For example, during the air-raids on London during World War II, the rate of intestinal perforations due to peptic ulcers rose dramatically among Londoners. The rate dropped to normal after the raids stopped.

Exceptions to this recovery scenario may include members of oppressed groups, whose oppression is part of the fabric of living. While true trauma ends or decreases, the underlying oppression continues. For many women in this study, their experience fell under the oppression model. When and if the abuse by their mothers ended, many of the daughters experienced further sexual, emotional and physical abuse. In addition to the intrafamilial oppression, many daughters reported that they experienced discrimination in education or employment, due to sexism and homophobia.

Second, unlike natural disasters and wars, a continuing traumatic experience such as sexual abuse is not public and collective, but private and hidden. Thus, survivors of sexual abuse have typically faced the extra burden of being the "holder" or "shield" of secret trauma. This long-term and unresolved stress has led to major mood problems for the daughters (these issues will be addressed more fully in a second volume on psychotherapy). According to their response, a large majority of the daughters experienced mood disturbances: 73% of the respondents reported childhood anxiety; 85% adult anxiety; 69% childhood depression; and 94% of the daughters reported adult depression.

The interplay between their traumatic abuse and the loss of their mothers' support, nurture and appropriate role modeling leads to high levels of life-long mood disturbances. The APA in *DSM-III-R* reports no specific data on adult anxiety, only that it is common. However, a history of depression is reported as occurring in 10% to 25% of adult females (APA, 1994, p. 341). These statistics make the adult rate for abused daughters of 94% staggering in comparison. If even half (47%) of the reported depression were clinically diagnosable and verified, the rate is still staggering.

Stress as an Outcome of the Trauma and Abuse

The abuse caused countless hours of the daughters' childhoods to be absorbed in the attempt to understand it and to recuperate from it emotionally, physically, and psychologically. The time spent trying to regain balance for the inner self consumes the time available for simply enjoying play and other joys of childhood. Trauma eats up time, energy and innocence.

Relatively high percentages of the daughters reported physical and behavioral symptoms of stress in their childhoods: 47% of the daughters experienced hypervigilance; 45% reported breathing problems; 41% suffered headaches; 38% of the respondents described heart pounding/racing; 27% took repetitive showers or baths; 25% experienced nausea; and 20% of the respondents described tightness in their throats.

Trauma also consumes peace of mind and a sense of safety, breeding self-destructiveness, as the respondents reported: 39% of the daughters engaged in childhood self-mutilation; 39% of them had made childhood suicidal gestures; and 31% of the survivors had made actual suicide attempts in childhood.

Also related to their stress levels was the amount of time children spent near their perpetrating mothers and the amount of time spent in the space where they were abused. In this population, nearly 100% of the survivors were abused in the bedroom, bathroom, living room, and kitchen. Imagine a daughter sexually abused by her mother in the bathroom then being told to clean that room. Entrapment at the scene of the abuse may account for some of the stress among the daughters.

Trouble Speaking: Childhood Speech Problems

Some respondents reported difficulties with speech: 12% of the abused daughters noted stuttering, and 7% wrote that they'd had "other speech problems." Some reported periods of muteness and others mute "inner children."

The APA (1994, p. 64) reports that 1% of children stutter and that it's more common among younger children. This survey didn't ask about adult stuttering, but it is a symptom that may yield information if pursued, and may be an indication of high stress levels related to enforced silence and secret keeping.

CHANGING THE PAINFUL REALITY: DISTORTION AND DISTRACTION PHENOMENA

True psychosis or mental illness has been regarded as relatively rare in children but is apparently being more commonly diagnosed. Children's symptoms and disorders in reaction to stress are more likely to be identified than previously.

The survey responses reveal incidence of two phenomena commonly considered symptoms of mental disturbances *in adults*: dissociative fantasies and hallucination. But I caution against concluding that adults who report the occurrence of such phenomena during their childhoods are mentally ill. Some respondents in this study have past diagnoses of psychosis, and some may have been truly psychotic. For now, it may be wiser to consider these data as indications of childhood stress symptoms.

Certain patterns and methods of distortion are used by these daughters as psychological defenses and/or coping mechanisms. *Fewer than 15% of the women in this study have had life-long, conscious memory of sexual abuse by their mothers.* These daughters developed self-protective mechanisms to reduce or deaden their physical, emotional and spiritual pain and to block recall of the abuse.

> I remembered almost nothing from ages 7 to 18.

Once adopted, these defenses often become a natural state for the survivors. A daughter may learn to numb her body, to *not* cry, or to *not* think about or remember the abuse. However, if these defenses become an ingrained and natural function, a daughter may not be able to feel or cry under any circumstances later, even when it would be an appropriate and healthy reaction to current events. Although these distortions may have been the best defense possible at the necessary moment, they may also become terribly isolating traps for the daughters in their adult years.

Magical Thinking

Thirty-six percent (36%) of the daughters in this group reported that they had engaged in childhood magical thinking, a normal occurrence for all children between ages three and five. In healthy development, magical thinking is outgrown and normally does not occur beyond appropriate ages. In contrast, I've treated adult clients abused by their mothers who still believed that they were born to other parents or families and switched in the hospital, or that there was someone who really loved them who would appear someday and rescue them. This fantasy life often occurred most fully while they were safely away from home, alone, during school, or awake in bed. This magical thinking may merge with fantasies that may become closely guarded adulthood secrets.

> I [did a lot] of day dreaming.

Imaginary Helpers

Twenty-five percent (25%) of the daughters developed imaginary and harmless playmates and helpers for support.

As a child I had "imaginary helpers." The real people in my life were unavailable.

While children who are not abused also create imaginary playmates who fill their lives with pleasure and support, these helpers are often still present for adult survivors in a mild form, especially during times of stress or need for emotional comfort. They can be a vivid presence or more like a favorite childhood doll rediscovered from time to time in its storage place, very familiar but from a different time. The reasons for reliance on such helpers are simple.

[I] created a fantasy story to put myself to sleep right after the abuse.

My sense of the way imaginary helpers work is that it shows the healing power of our minds — help when no other help is in sight. I think that you might find that among those women who had imaginary helpers, coping and adjustment through life is significantly better.

Imaginary helpers are often like siblings who "live" with the survivor and know about the abuse. Needed for comfort and companionship during unsafe periods, they may not have been needed, for example, at school. The imaginary helpers often "go into hiding" at about the time the children realize how truly unsafe their lives are.

Withdrawal Into Fantasy and Hallucination

Fifty-nine percent (59%) of the daughters reported they lived in a fantasy world for at least part of childhood. Their degree of withdrawal varied. For some respondents, it was a profound disconnection from reality and likely caused problems; for others, it was a well-developed ability to escape trauma.

[I'd cope by] concentrating on an object nearby.

Eighteen percent (18%) report hallucinations during childhood, including seeing, hearing, smelling and/or tasting things that were not present.

One respondent remembers looking out her bedroom window as a child and seeing things "float by." She recalls seeing fragments of body parts or animals outside the window. Her description sounds like the drawings commonly done by dissociative individuals. As an adult, she is astounded that these occurrences seemed "so normal" at the time and is disturbed to know she could so calmly engage in this phenomenon. Another daughter reports:

> [It was] related to hallucinations — but much more a whole inner world would take over — colors, sounds, etc. As a youngster I considered this my basic wrongness.

Fifteen percent (15%) of the daughters reported occasional auditory hallucinations such as hearing voices.

> I heard voices only when I was 10 years old — the age of the most severe abuse by my mother and father.

Visual and auditory hallucinations were frequently desperate attempts to cope with difficult situations. However, when and if an adult daughter enters a regressive state and/or remembers these phenomena, it is often so disturbing she may express concerns about the soundness of her mental health.

Mild hallucinatory phenomena commonly include hearing, seeing and smelling things not present and feeling touched when alone. Some hallucinations have a biochemical cause and may need to be treated with medication if they are too frequent, severe, or disruptive. In my clinical experience, most hallucinatory sensations indicate unresolved emotional issues pushing to be addressed at the conscious level. These hallucinations often occur in the form of flashbacks in adulthood, reported by 90% of the daughters.

Survivors who experience flashbacks — intense visual, auditory, tactile, olfactory, or taste-related re-experiencing of sensations from the past — may fear that they are "going crazy." One survivor reports:

> I used to hear voices when I was diagnosed psychotic. I still [hear them] during flashbacks, smell things that connect to memories and hear my mother's voice and see her face telling me to shut up when I talk about the abuse. Also I see her face very angry when I let myself feel my feelings during flashbacks.

These occurrences can be very unsettling and frightening, especially if the survivor does not remember their source in childhood abuse. However, these occurrences make sense once the source is known and the daughter understands it is a memory breaking through to consciousness. They are like coded messages from inside ourselves, even if the experiences may feel like they're coming from outside.

Perhaps by way of distraction, 60% of the abused daughters became adult "work-aholics." Devoting an inordinate amount of time to work could be considered a need to stay very busy and focused as a way to avoid emotions. This excessive devotion to work may first appear as early school achievement and/or heightened levels of school and social activities. School itself may have the effect of encouraging constant productivity. For some mother-abused daughters, such productivity may have become a defense against looking inward. This activity may be the beginning of charting a course away from childhood and into adulthood.

IMPAIRED ATTENTION AND LEARNING

Aside from how well or poorly an individual thinks, the ability to stay "on task" while trying to think is important. Forty percent (40%) report they had childhood attention-span problems. Sixteen percent (16%) say they were hyperactive in childhood. Seventeen percent (17%) said they feel they have attention deficit disorder.

The APA (1994) recognizes a childhood condition called Attention-Deficit Hyperactivity Disorder (ADHD) which it reports occurs in 3% to 5% of American children (p. 82). Attention span problems (40%) and hyperactivity (16%) are components of ADHD; in this survey these two symptoms appeared at levels several times higher than normal. These self-reports are not necessarily diagnoses of ADHD, but they indicate that the survivors experienced frequent problems in this area.

Forty-seven percent (47%) of the daughters reported being hypervigilant in childhood. Some daughters lived with situations where it was not safe to be engrossed in a book or in learning. Their need to stay vigilant and aware of others in their environment impeded their ability to relax and focus.

Some daughters did well in school but could not study at home. These problems can become so ingrained that even in adulthood, they cannot focus without anxiety except under specific circumstances. Often as childhood problems are resolved, there is dramatic improvement in both performance and focus.

The Overwhelmed Student: Trouble with School

When asked about their school experiences, a significant number reported problems.

Childhood school problems	**23%**
School disruption	**19%**
Delayed achievement	**28%**
Low school achievement	**31%**

Problems with school emerged for some daughters when elements of their abuse experiences at home were also experienced in school.

> [I was] very quiet and blend(ed) into the woodwork so as not to be noticed except to do well at school.

> I got kicked out of school for swearing at a teacher who was humiliating another kid in front of the entire class. I hated him and my mother for doing that.

The daughters often had very low tolerance for behaviors by others that create the responses they had to their abuse.

Some survivors of sexual abuse by their mothers struggle with attention and focusing problems which may negatively affect both home and school lives, including the ability to learn, remember and recall information and experience. Research is needed on the interplay of attention deficit problems in abusive mothers and their daughters. Some early studies suggest that mothers with attention deficit disorders touch their children less frequently than mothers without such disorders. Children with short attention spans who are hyperactive may enhance any attention and impulsiveness problems in their mothers. If both mother and child have attention disorders, that could lead to untold difficulties. For example, to get attention-disordered mothers and children to focus positive attention on each other, in the right mood, at the right time, and in the right frame of mind may be unlikely in some cases, leading to neglect.

Making It Go Away: Cognitive Distortion

Abusive experiences may create a lingering disturbance in the daughters' ability to think about the sexual abuse by their mothers. They may either distort the reality of their abusive experience or distract themselves from awareness of it. This distortion occurs primarily through a "block" in the freedom to think, which begins in childhood and continues into adulthood, and psychological defenses such as denial, repression, or dissociation.

Thinking About the Unthinkable: Difficulty Thinking About Abuse

In response to the question,"Do you find it difficult to allow yourself to think about the abuse now?" 70% of the respondents said yes, 24% said no, and 4% of them wrote that they were unsure. Some added comments:

Mom had to die before I could remember it.

IT IS STILL DIFFICULT FOR ME TO BELIEVE THAT MY MOTHER IS A HUMAN BEING AND NOT A MONSTER.

As children, the daughters learned to distort what they could not control or escape.

Many of these daughters are experienced in working on incest and family issues related to sexual abuse by males, but find it very difficult to focus on the sexual abuse by their mothers.

Respondents' difficulties in thinking about the abuse do not necessarily interfere with other areas of cognitive functioning. They are often highly trained and focused in other areas of their lives. Some daughters I've met or talked with on the phone are stunningly intelligent, articulate and intellectually vital. They often display remarkable curiosity and tenacity in resolving this issue. The inability to focus on sexual abuse by their mothers has nothing to do with intelligence, but rather requires the emotional freedom to think about it.

It is very hard to look at and think about, much less talk about. The feelings of betrayal are far worse than in abuse by a father.

Some abused daughters have lost their clarity to difficulties such as alcohol or posttraumatic stress.

Recall is very hard because it ruptures the primary relationship in life — like being orphaned.

This rupture causes a cognitive and emotional collision point for the daughters: their socialization about mothers, homosexuality, female sexuality, their need for an idealized mother figure, or their knowledge of society's harsh judgments conflict as they try to think about being sexually abused by their mothers. They are faced with thinking the unthinkable. The stakes are very high until the survivors know they can cope with the pressure.

According to the daughters' comments, the distortion is an effort to *hold off the pain* of accepting reality and prevent the feared changes that may accompany conscious knowledge.

> It's so hard to get to [these memories]. After years of dealing with the abuse by my father, which covered many years and was at times violent, I am still terrified of really "taking on" the abuse by my mom. With her it probably only happened 3 or 4 times over a 5 or 6 years period. I am still horrified by the dependency, terror, rage, and overwhelming sexual excitement embedded in those memories. The idea of going back in and knowing this reality is still terrifying, and the fear of really knowing is complicated by the incredible fear of losing her once I know.

When the survivor clears any cognitive barriers and can think at will about her experience, the next barrier may be the pain of *accepting the reality of the abuse*. Seventy-six percent (76%) report they have difficulty believing the abuse happened. Nineteen percent (19%) say continued belief is not a problem.

> This is a MAJOR problem.

They may flee from their own knowledge.

> At first it seemed too bizarre.

> How difficult it is to believe that it happened and how much more subtle it is than father/daughter sexual abuse. How much longer it takes for it to come to the conscious mind than abuse by a male. How much more vulnerable the client feels dealing with mother's abuse than father's abuse.

> [I find it] difficult to accept it as a reality and that it was intentional. Being unsure of everything that happened gives all my life a feeling of unreality.

> It has shaken up my view of reality so much it gives me the creeps.

Some daughters have memories, but experience difficulty remembering any feeling or emotion.

I have pictures but no feelings. The memories are only partial.

☐

Mostly the feelings are hard to remember.

Some daughters distort their reality by using mild to severe dissociation, a defense mechanism that blocks awareness. This distortion may cause forgetting almost as soon as memories become conscious.

Sometimes I talk about it in the 3rd person. My therapist calls it dissociative. In other words, I split.

The inability to clearly picture the abuse experience and freely explore its meaning can be frustrating.

I go back to the [jigsaw] puzzle image and of trying to put it together and it feels like the border has been in place for quite awhile. All the memories and knowledge of my past have come to the surface…if not all a big portion anyway. But now it feels like I've found a pattern to make sense out of all the scrambled pieces in the middle. [That part is] all the impact of my past on who I am now, who I'm going to be, and how to manage that. It might be just a beginning but at least it doesn't feel like I'm trying to put the puzzle together with the [middle] pieces upside down anymore.

Sixty percent (60%) of the 93 survey respondents report adult confusion related to the abuse by their mothers. Two respondents wrote:

At about age 25 I noticed that I was having trouble concentrating and that I had difficulty remembering things such as phone numbers, appointments, and plots of books I'd just read. No one I talked with seemed too concerned or very ready with an explanation.

☐

It's difficult to identify due to the confusion of mothering roles and responsibilities, [physical care] and sexual arousal [which may be very covert as in my case]. There is great confusion on the survivor's part due to [her] natural mothering role in a child's life. It's sometimes harder for the child to interpret this type of incest as abusive, as it is easier for a mother to be covertly sexually abusive than for a father.

Confusing and deceiving the daughters about the abusive behaviors may have been a deliberate tactic by some of the mothers. By creating confusion, the mothers have more power.

Confusion about right and wrong, from her whimsical contradictions and her refusal to acknowledge my reality.

This respondent remembers that her mother saw her father and a brother sexually abuse her during childhood but her mother would never acknowledge it. Another says:

After the period during which all the incest occurred [with mother and her brother], my mother married "up" into the middle class. It was like we won the Megabucks. There was no discussion of the trauma or transition into our new life, a real classic "geographic cure." We moved to a city and then my mother began a campaign of terror against me, calling me "crazy," hauling me off to a shrink to be "fixed," locking me in my room for weeks at a time — real <u>heavy</u> emotional abuse.

Naturally, I did indeed become "crazy" as she wished and developed many symptoms as listed above. I now believe that she did this deliberately in order to discredit me in advance should I talk about what went on in [our former home].

I was 10 years old and kind of a blabbermouth. I was a loose cannon on deck and her position in the middle class was threatened by my presence. Most of the symptoms [I've noted on the survey] are the result of her campaign, but I believe they are indirectly related to the incest for the reasons I've described.

Because of the mother being in the care-taker role, I think it's the easiest [abuse] to cover up. At times [it is hard] even for the child to realize it is wrong.

A Threatening World:
Hypervigilance, Anxiety, Fear and Phobias

Forty-seven percent (47%) of the abused daughters reported childhood hypervigilance, and 57% of the daughters experience it as adults. The increase may be due to revictimization, but its basis is undoubtedly the childhood abuse. This kind of watchfulness is not just normal alertness but more like a disturbing need to know what's happening at all times, an attempt to have a small measure of control over the environment.

An unsurprising 73% of respondents reported childhood anxiety. For many, the persistent boundary-crossing and violence provided a valid basis for such anxiety.

I learned early that she could be very violent and I got very good at "reading" the tension level in the house, watching for even the most subtle clues that she was getting agitated. I sometimes hated it when she was calm and I would be anxious when she was sullen. It made her too hard to read. When she'd finally explode verbally you had to get out fast or freeze so she wouldn't focus on you. But if you were her target there was no stopping her. It could go on for hours. My dad would ignore it until it spilled over onto him and then he'd tell her to stop to protect himself. I had little respect for either of them and I spent too much time raging at her inside myself. Now I don't hate her anymore but I think she was a waste of a life and then she died.

175

The abuse produced some unique dilemmas that may be the causes of some reported anxiety.

> I have wanted her to die. When I was younger I was <u>very</u> concerned that she might die.

Thirty-three (33%) of the respondent daughters reported childhood phobias. Some of these fears have very clear causes while others seem less formed and focused. The cause may be totally unknown even to the phobic person. Phobias are often symbolic fears that individuals find safer to experience than the real threat. For example, it might feel safer to fear a big dog than to be consciously aware of a dangerous person who had caused harm or who might do so now.

The daughters reported several kinds of phobias, and 84% reported childhood fears related to the sexual abuse.

> [I have a] fear of heights and claustrophobia.

> [I am] sort of phobic of things that cause flashbacks.

> I wouldn't say I'm compulsive — but almost. I have an over-awareness of germs.

> [I had] fear that she could read my mind and would punish me for [what I thought of her]. Fear of abandonment if I did not comply with her wishes and demands. Needed to be absolutely PERFECT, and still feeling inadequate.

> No one knew of my fear. [I was] too afraid to tell.

Reactions to original fears such as hypervigilance and possible anxiety attacks may continue into their adulthood.

> [I have] unspecific, free floating fears of others [about] what they want from me

Fifty-seven percent (57%) of the daughters report being hypervigilant in adulthood, a significant increase over their 47% reported level during childhood. When the mother is the abuser and has unlimited access to the daughter day and night, hypervigilance becomes highly likely. Children expend a lot of energy to maintain high levels of tense watchfulness.

[I] hate background noises that distract me from being able to be fully alert to what's happening around me — like a lawnmower outside the window or a loud fan.
I can hear a cat walk on carpeting.
I can hear my son's car 3 blocks away.
I hear clocks ticking that the OWNERS have never heard.
Scares people.

Minimizing

The survey did not ask specifically about minimizing, but the following statements illustrate a conflict: often the intellect says yes, but the emotions say no. The minimizing appears to reduce the drain on the emotions.

I minimize the abuse … "mine wasn't that bad!" and many of us fantasize and can't see reality. It happens! Ignoring it assures that its impact will resurrect in some other area of your life.

The abuse by my mother was <u>very</u> subtle. There was no oral-genital contact. Because it seems so "mild" I often have difficulty believing I was sexually abused. However, her behavior was clearly sexual. It doesn't take much to damage a child. It's not just motherly affection.

I have only one memory of an event relating to sexual abuse, but I filled this out because I feel it happened to me and I can relate to many of the symptoms and effects.

Idealizing

Thirty-six percent (36%) of the daughters engaged in idealizing as a defense during childhood, and 44% of them use it as adults.

I idealized my father as a way of coping with the abuse. I had great pain in finally facing that he wasn't really there for me as a protector or advocate. He took care of his own emotional needs first.

The daughters may be vulnerable to idealizing individuals because they often feel betrayed by social institutions such as the churches, the media, the mental health system and, for some, even the women's and self-help movements.

Denial

Seventy-two percent (72%) of the daughters report they engage in denial about the abuse.

> I feel it is much more subtle, there is less physical evidence (semen, pubic hairs, etc.), so much more possibility for denial. I think it is possible for it to have happened to you without you ever realizing the sources of your pain.

> It's the last thing I ever want to know. When I was 26 and very depressed — but without incest memories or therapy — I could not stand my mother's continual insistence that I fix her life, so I left the country and stayed away for 9½ years. I would have gone to the moon if I could. I would have denied it forever. The denial is incredible.

SUFFER THE LITTLE CHILDREN: RELIGION AND ABUSE

Religion was a comfort to a few, but some recognize they became lost in religion as a way to cope with their abuse or they found their religious leanings thwarted by abuse issues.

> [I had] religious fanaticism. I wanted to go join a convent when I was 7.

> After my dad, who had sexually abused me, died when I was 12, I threw myself into religion. I was going to become a nun, I went to church and prayed at recesses and noon hours everyday. I helped a nun clean after school. This also allowed me to avoid spending time with other classmates, where I felt I didn't belong, and to not go home so soon. When I fantasized about running away, I thought about going to the church, hiding by the big basement windows, and the nuns finding me.

Twenty-five percent (25%) of the daughters reported an overuse of religion in adulthood as a way to deny or resolve the abuse issues. Although religion may have been a genuine comfort for some, it has been a deadening trap for others.

Sexual abuse by mothers occurs in all major racial and religious groups (see Table 8), but these data do not indicate conclusively that such abuse is more prevalent in one group than others. This information is drawn from respondents who received mental health treatment and who may have attended mother-daughter incest seminars. The availability of

Table 8

RELIGIOUS AFFILIATION OF RESPONDENTS

Protestant	27 (29%)
Catholic	14 (15%)
Jewish	6 (7%)
Other	42 (45%)

treatment, support groups, education, and freedom to speak of sexual matters regarding mothers varies from culture to culture.

Twenty-four percent (24%) of the respondents reported that they had shifted away from their childhood religious affiliations during adulthood. This shift may be important because mothers are often the initiators and teachers of early religious training. For these daughters, leaving their childhood religion may be an act of autonomy. However, such a move may also leave a sense of loss and incompleteness, but some respondents search for greater spiritual involvement.

At one time or another Protestant and Catholic [but now I'm an] agnostic.

By birth — half Jewish and half Catholic. [Now] Protestant.

Seeing what's there, just trying to follow inner guidance to a greater good, influence of Buddhist, Native American, pagan and new age teachings.

I cannot think of an individual I've communicated with who was sexually abused by her mother who indicated that religion or a church was supportive in their recovery. Religious faith is personal and private, but none said it provided strength.

> Feeling like a mere assemblage of parts I put together, rather than a whole person. I feel I have no soul and that's why my religious faith has suffered. I'm lacking the main receptor for God — my soul.

> Incest is also damaging to one's religious development. It destroys children's faith in life and any possibility of cosmic spirituality. Parents are god images and if parents are acting in an evil way, children despair, psychologically and spiritually, as well as trying to become the scapegoat.

The daughters have frequently become very adept at various kinds of distortion as a way of coping with their abuse, but they may be unaware of how automatic it has become. One therapeutic goal would be to reach such a level of awareness that they can begin to make an informed choice about how to deal with it now.

DOING THE BEST THEY COULD: POSITIVE COPING

Despite the harm they experienced and the disruption of their cognitive and emotional development they reported as being related to being abused by their mothers, some daughters found positive ways to cope.

The Good Student: Achievement in School

Some daughters found safety at school and excelled. School may have been the first safe environment they experienced. The school environment, with its rules, boundaries, and rewards, may have provided a reliable structure and a sense of safety that came as a profound relief. Some daughters had become "little adults," so the teachers often responded well to them. One survivor described math and spelling as a wonderful stabilizing force in her life.

> Four plus four equaled eight which was true yesterday, it is true today, and it will be true tomorrow. I love the order of those kind of rules.

School may have been the first safe haven for many children abused by their mothers. Although some were initially wary of school, some daughters found they loved the safety, structure and basic fairness of most elementary school classrooms. School may have been their retreat from painful family life. Rather than school being a part of the child's life it may have been the focus and core. School may have provided a place to feel secure or to hide.

> I was free when I was in school…9 AM to 3 PM daily or Sundays at church. [And] there was less [abuse] when she went to work when I was 12.

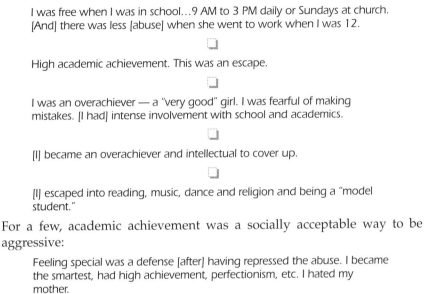

> High academic achievement. This was an escape.

> I was an overachiever — a "very good" girl. I was fearful of making mistakes. [I had] intense involvement with school and academics.

> [I] became an overachiever and intellectual to cover up.

> [I] escaped into reading, music, dance and religion and being a "model student."

For a few, academic achievement was a socially acceptable way to be aggressive:

> Feeling special was a defense [after] having repressed the abuse. I became the smartest, had high achievement, perfectionism, etc. I hated my mother.

> [I was into] perfectionism, high/over achievement in school.

The academic achievement of these 93 women reflects the important role school played. Several reported they developed emotional problems and could no longer avoid the effects of the abuse when they reached the end of their academic training.

Had I surveyed 93 women prisoners or very low-income women, I suspect the level of educational achievement, positive reinforcement and school acceptance would have been much lower. However, I don't know that there would be any difference in intelligence in such a group. Little girls sexually abused by their mothers are very vulnerable. How they are treated in educational settings may make an enormous difference in their lives. The following daughter was fortunate.

> I was very badly abused by the time I began kindergarten and the idea of going to school was terrifying because by then I don't think I trusted anyone. My mother often told and retold a story of how she had to "whip her (my) ass all the way to school" for several days before I'd go willingly, and she always said, "but by god she went." Well, I'd been beaten at home and on my way to school. Even at five I could figure out where my best option lay. I never got whipped at school.

> I did well in elementary school but my mother resented the acceptance and support I received from my teachers. She'd call me "teacher's pet" and tell me my grades were good only because I was the teacher's "favorite." Fortunately there were others who encouraged me which helped to balance her active discouragement. "You think you're so smart," she'd sneer.

> Finally I think I just cut her off as an ignorant, rejecting asshole. At the end of high school I was to receive several awards and the school made a big deal of inviting my parents to a banquet as if they had much to do with my academic success. I'd signed my own report cards half the time. I felt betrayed. I just wanted to get away from them by that age.

> I went to college in the fall and promptly flunked out. There was a lot of pain. It took me years to get a degree.

School success is not just a matter of intelligence, and little girls abused by their mothers, confused about adults and trust, tempted to withdraw and accepted if they do, are vulnerable in our current educational system.

In addition to finding escape, safety, constructive role models and self-esteem in school settings, some daughters found other ways to get some of their emotional needs met in positive ways.

Finding a New Home: Adoption Into Another Family

Forty-three percent (43%) of the daughters report they experienced an emotional "adoption" into another family. They simply found a different family, as two respondents reported:

> We moved frequently and I adopted a new mother figure wherever I lived.

> Sort of ... [there] was an older woman with a lot of pets to play with next door.

Such informal adoptions can become a pattern for getting their emotional needs met.

> This happened in my adulthood, too.

Animals were another important source of comfort because they gave consistent affection for some children, as reported by one daughter:

> I adopted animals as my family.

Exorcizing Demons Through Exercise: Intense Athletic Involvement

Eighteen percent (18%) report intense involvement in athletics during childhood or adolescence. Such activity likely served as a legitimate reason to be absent from the home, as a way to get aggressions out, and a source of reliable systems of rules and rewards. These may have been far more trustworthy than the people in their lives. In addition, the tension relief athletics provide can be a safe activity affording companionship without emotional intimacy. Very intense athletic activity also may make a girl's body look distinctly different from her mother's.

Clearly, the daughters in this study learned a variety of ways to cope with their very difficult situations and developed skills, distortions and abilities that might not have been developed without the trauma. The major question for most is how they want to deal with the trauma now. Are there other and perhaps better ways available to them now that were not available earlier?

Part Five

DAUGHTERS' RESPONSES TO THE ABUSE

CHAPTER 12

Signposts of Violation:
The Emotional, Behavioral and Physical Aftermath

esponses to childhood sexual abuse may be expressed in emotional, behavioral or physical symptoms. These symptoms may be directed inward against the self or out toward others. The daughters who responded to this survey showed both of these responses.

Hurt Inside: Inward Symptoms

Possibly the most prevalent effect of child sexual abuse of all kinds is damage to the child's self-esteem. Ninety-five percent (95%) of the daughters reported that they had self-esteem issues either in childhood and adolescence or continuing into their adult lives.

[I had] poor self esteem and found it hard to believe anyone valued me.

> Everyone also needs to know that sexual abuse does unfathomable damage. When I look at Rorschach responses of children who have been abused I see that black empty pit of worthlessness and pain and rage. It's already there even if the child is only 3–4 years old and can't talk about the abuse. It doesn't matter if the abuse is violent or seductive it still eats a person from the inside out.

Some daughters cannot fend off enmeshment. With unlimited access to the child, the mother takes so much of a child's energy that the child fails to become a confident, well established separate self.

> [I feel] emptiness and grief at the loss of self.

If the child is later rejected by the mother, clinical experience suggests that she may spend her energies attempting to re-establish fusion with her mother.

Self-esteem can be damaged by feeling stigmatized, different, other, and not normal. Forty-seven percent (47%) of these abused daughters felt stigmatized as children.

> Feeling not OK and not like everyone else.

> I felt total isolation from " normal" people.

The daughters reported feelings of esteem-damaging shame due to the abuse, and the degree of shame varied among the daughters.

> [I have] shame based behaviors and shame based isolation and guilt.

> [I sometimes] have pathological sweating from feelings of extreme shame and disgustingness.

Daughters of sexually abusive mothers may also feel shame because they cannot love their mothers. Positive counters to shame include contact with others who've had similar experiences and validation for a refusal to carry the responsibility for others' behaviors. The daughters may need to hear clearly from others: "You didn't do it. You did not cause the abuse to occur. It's not your fault." As one respondent emphatically wrote:

> OVERCOMING THE SENSE OF SHAME IS IMPOSSIBLE UNLESS OTHER PEOPLE BELIEVE AND SUPPORT ME (WHICH, FORTUNATELY, THEY HAVE).

These daughters all lost a major source of normal socialization through either the mothers' dysfunctional behaviors or the daughters' rejection of (and/or withdrawal from) their mothers as role models. Consequently, the daughters often are unsure what constitutes "normal" behavior, thoughts, and desires.

> [I remember] wishing I could be a "regular little girl" [and] not knowing why I wasn't.

Some daughters reported that by mid-childhood they were suffering observable damage to their personalities, but for some the damage was mitigated by their ability to see that their mothers had the problem. This clarity of perception diminished the influence their mothers had on them, for better or worse. However, few daughters who experienced sexual abuse with their mothers could ward off all damage without significant outside intervention (for an example, see p. 190).

EMOTIONAL SYMPTOMS

Emotional symptoms in survivors of childhood sexual abuse commonly occur either as emotional constriction or absence, or as intrusive emotions beyond the survivor's control.

Shutting Down: Emotional Constriction

Responses to this survey indicate one effect of keeping the abuse secret may be the daughters' apparent absence of emotion. It may become difficult for a daughter to feel, understand or express emotions. In addition, some daughters may not realize they are emotionally shut down because they have lived with their emotional constriction for so long that it feels normal to them.

> [I am] unable to laugh or express feelings.

> Rather than physical "lack of feeling" I experience emotional lack of feeling. NO interest in life, wondering why people get so excited about life even though I force myself to do all the things I "should."

> I don't/can't cry. I am afraid (irrationally, of course) that I'll die if I cry, have sex, wear a costume, shout, say " no" when I'm angry …

HELP FROM OUTSIDE:
A Successful Intervention

The most successful interventions were by grandparents, but unfortunately there were very few. One set of grandparents removed their granddaughter at age two from her abusive mother's care and raised her as their child. There were two critical elements to this successful intervention:

1. This daughter's mother was obviously mentally ill, and the daughter knew and understood that all her life. The other adults in her life supported and validated that perception. This respondent, therefore, had less need to distort the reality of the abuse, and the abusive experiences were not hidden within her as confusion or fear.

2. The daughter strongly believes she was loved and valued by other important adults in her life. It is also perhaps significant that of all the respondents she seems to believe the most strongly that she was loved, valued and protected by a male (her grandfather).

What a fortunate little girl she was.

Helpless Explosions: Uncontrolled Emotions

Some daughters' emotions exploded against their will, intruding into their lives and sometimes leading to other problems.

[I remember] crying or laughing uncontrollably [during childhood].

I would try to control my emotions but sometimes she would harass me verbally until I would eventually explode with rage. I knew that if I did that [explode] she would get physically aggressive with me. I hated the bitch. She would go at me for hours and then if I pushed back verbally she'd explode, too. I learned to just do it, make her explode, get it over with. When I was young I couldn't stop or control it myself. After awhile I'd call her a name and she'd go crazy. There'd be physical violence and it would be over with, things would be calmer. It was better to set her off and get it over with than to just take it by the hour. After I left home and she'd call I'd just hang up on her. But the first few times I did it I would tremble and break into a sweat.

Such out-of-control emotions often raise the fear among survivors that they are crazy, insane. Half (50%) of these respondents reported fearing that they were "going crazy" during childhood, and 67% feared it during adulthood. Some respondents appear to fear they're "infected" with their mothers' mental health problems and that they too might become "crazy."

The survey posed questions about feelings of anger and rage due to the abuse. Half the respondents reported that they felt anger during childhood (50%), increasing markedly in adulthood (74%). Reports of rage also increased significantly from childhood (52%) to adulthood (63%). Thirty-three percent (33%) of the daughters also reported feeling "hostile" about the abuse during childhood.

Tremendous temper tantrums and feeling evil and deviant.

I thought about sharpening the end of a broom stick, soaking it in alcohol so it would really sting, and ramming it up her rectum and vagina.

Such feelings can begin at very young ages, and some abused daughters cannot remember a time when they were not angry at their mothers. However, given common social and cultural demands on little girls to be docile and compliant, it was no doubt difficult for them to show anger or hostility. Daughters reported still feeling the need to attempt to bury, hide or deny their rage as adults, and some entered psychotherapy as initially hostile clients. As one daughter wrote:

> It's impossible to overestimate the depth of rage, despair, and denial in the mother-abused client. The longing for a good mother is a howling need from the soul of the person. Be aware that this client grew up with no safety net, betrayed from the very start, at the very core. It must be very hard to be such a person's therapist. Expect a lot of "bad" behavior as the lonely, betrayed child emerges.

This anger and hostility can spill over into other relationships, creating for these daughters a deeply disturbing difficulty in relating to others.

> At times [I'm] verbally abusive of other adults close to me.

While their rage may be in some sense rational (having a basis in the reality of their sexual abuse), its effect on their adult lives may be unwelcome and yet prolonged, as this daughter wrote:

> Probably the most painful and lingering aspect of the abuse is that my rage toward my mother frightens other people. I don't want to frighten anyone.

> I only want to SURVIVE. And if I bury my rage, if I am silent, if I am passive, I agree to perpetuate the great lie of my mother's life — that she is a good mother — and I agree to live in the world of fear and shame she created for me.

> I also want to live in reality, to trust and to love, and to create a trusting world where human beings are valued.

To Kill the Perpetrator: Homicidal Ideation

There were no specific survey questions about homicide, but some daughters wrote about it.

> [You might have asked about] homicidal ideation, about killing mother or mother's death.

The following statement is from a gracious, warm, intelligent, and lovely woman I met who later identified herself as a respondent.

> Did you protect your mother?
> Why didn't you kill yourself?
> Why don't you kill her now?
> Did the other parent know?
> Do you like yourself now?
> Do you ever have a nice day?

For some daughters, homicidal ideation began in childhood when they became enraged and frustrated with the sexual and other forms of abuse they experienced. Some of them developed fairly specific homicidal ideas and urges, as one writes:

> [I had a] desire to kill her with a butcher knife.

These daughters' statements show how strong and prolonged these emotions and thoughts can be, but also reveal the futility some sexually abused daughters feel:

> [The] rage is volcanic and never disappears, only smolders. I would have killed her if I thought ANYONE would understand and not send me to jail. As long as she never apologizes to me or acknowledges that it happened, I'll wish her dead.

> I wish I could kill her but it wouldn't solve her problem. I still hate her and don't know how to stop.

Despite these thoughts, in reality, the daughters' destructive actions are most often directed towards themselves rather than toward their mothers.

Embedded Pain: Hurting the Self

The daughters' frustration and anger as children may have resulted in destructive behaviors either turned inward on themselves or outward into the social environment. These feelings were often related to depression and anxiety and may have become deeply ingrained in the daughters' lives, reappearing during unrelated occurrences of depression, anxiety, or stress. They also vary with each daughter in degree and seriousness.

Seventy percent (70%) of the respondents reported adult self-destructive behaviors, and 65% reported self-defeating behaviors, such as self-punishment or demonstrations of emotional pain.

> [I] stayed in a horrible marriage for 26 years. [I] sabotage myself in any good thing.

> I continue to have sexual/anger problems with women approximately my mother's age. I seek them out and then go through the whole love-sex-anger-fear cycle I lived with my mother. I'm dying for a mother.

By honestly and clearly exploring their underlying true needs, the daughters apparently learn to understand and manage such behaviors.

Thirty-nine percent (39%) of the abused daughters reported self-mutilations in childhood, and 34% reported adult self-mutilation. The childhood self-mutilation I've been told about involves primarily disfiguring, cutting of skin with sharp objects, or self-wounding through "accidents" such as breaking dishes or "tattooing" with ink pens. Burning skin is also common.

[I] was a self mutilator [through cutting] of my arms.

Chronic nose picking and any kind of scab picking — a bit extreme and a bit self-destructive. Usually at night.

Self-mutilation may become part of complex and deeply rooted patterns such as the one described here:

This tension $\longrightarrow$ pain/damage $\longrightarrow$ relief cycle that I experience today is in response to the maternal introject derived from an actual, historical experience (years of experience) of feeling an agonizing tension as I anticipated my mother's abuse of me. The waiting was so painful that I wanted to get the dreaded stuff over with. The waiting was torment. So now today, when I feel inner tension or discomfort, I yearn for pain: doesn't getting hurt always come in between tension or discomfort and relief???

Although self-mutilation frequently takes an active form, it can also be subtle, as this daughter suggests:

I suspect [self-mutilation] with my excess weight.

In addition to any self-mutilation scars, 14% reported scars from the physical abuse by their mothers. Scars left by the mothers may cause great shame and serve the daughters as visible proof of the abuse and confirm their feelings of being unloved.

Stopping the Pain:
Suicidal Thoughts, Gestures, and Attempts

There are four aspects of suicidal tendencies to consider regarding these daughters: 1) thinking about suicide (ideation); 2) making a suicidal gesture, but not wanting to die; 3) attempting suicide without success; 4) completing a suicide intentionally or unintentionally (of course, without corroborating evidence such as reports of abuse in suicide notes, there is no way to measure the incidence of suicide due to sexual abuse). Most of the daughters responding to this survey noted that they had thought about suicide both in childhood and as adults. More than a third (39%) had made suicidal gestures in childhood, while just under half (45%) had made such gestures as adults. Almost a third (31%) of the daughters had made suicide attempts in childhood, about the same proportion as did during their adult lives (32%).

The frequency of childhood suicide attempts in this sample is consistent with my clinical practice, personal experience and communication with survivors. The childhood incidence of suicidal ideation and gestures was likely higher than the data indicate. If this survey had asked about suicidal ideation and gestures directly, the data might show their incidence to be very high in the adults.

You might have asked about suicidal ideation [more directly].

[I have] chronic suicidal ideation.

Lots of suicidal ideation but no attempts. [I used to] think if I held my breath I could die. I wanted to.

The number of comments about self-destructive behaviors and thoughts of death indicate that they were important aspects of some daughters' childhood experiences. These patterns and thoughts may have been well established before the daughters were old enough to be rational about them or make reasoned choices.

Many of the abused daughters may have started down a path of anger, rage and self-destructive behaviors in childhood and as teens still had few good options for escaping their homes and/or perpetrators. They may have felt trapped, and if they attempted to get help they were often not served well. If actual or attempted sexual contacts by the mother continued, the daughter may have become desperate. Society offered little comfort or insight then, and precious little more now.

I made a suicide attempt at 13. Part of this was because I did not want to be a woman and also because I thought I was a lesbian. I knew there was something sexual between me and other women. I did not understand it. I was not attached to women. But there was "something" there. [I entered therapy at 13] and my therapist said I was "homo-erotic" but he never wanted to talk about the possibility of incest. He tried to give me drugs but I refused.

I was suicidal from 13 years old until adulthood.

195

Thoughts of death and suicide may become habitual and follow the daughter into adulthood:

> Prior to hospitalization there were thoughts of suicide, serious thoughts and calls to both [my] therapist and "hotlines" rather than real attempts or gestures. [It] did not go beyond thoughts, plans, [and] a yearning to be gone.

> [My] self esteem and self confidence are very low. Unsure if I can heal. I want to never struggle with suicidal thoughts again; yet they occur with regularity and the despair overwhelms me.

> [I] made several suicide attempts.

> My last suicide attempt when my heart stopped 3 times is what drove me to sobriety and the therapist I have now. I thought suicide was my only way out of my abuse and the pain.

This tendency toward suicide is disturbing; I cannot view these data without thinking that I know there are many women who died by their own hands to end this pain.

EXPRESSING THE PAIN: ACTING OUT BEHAVIORS

All of the daughters' answers to survey questions on acting-out behaviors — especially emotional, physical, or sexual abuse they may have perpetrated — are subject to the usual caveats regarding self-reports of illegal and socially unacceptable acts. In addition, we have already seen that many of the daughters are disgusted by any resemblance between them and their abusing mothers, so admitting to engaging in similar behaviors may be emotionally difficult — fraught with a sense of shame — or impossible, despite the safeguard of anonymity in this survey.

The daughters reported that 15% of them *physically* abused others in childhood, and 5% revealed that their physical abuse of other children amounted to torture. As adults, 10% of the daughters reported that they had physically abused children, and 7% had physically abused other adults.

Acts of aggression against children seem to decrease as the daughters reach adulthood — some respondents avoid children because they fear abusing them. These figures represent a self-reported 50% decrease in physical aggression against children between childhood and adulthood. In this sample, this decrease may reflect the daughters' increasing insight into their own issues and their efforts not to pass on the pain.

More research is needed to see the levels of continuing abuse in broader samples. Sixty-five percent (65%) of the daughters reported being *physically* abused by their mothers as part of their sexual abuse. How might they be controlling any aggressive urges they may currently have?

Fifteen percent (15%) of the daughters reported that in adulthood they had *emotionally* abused a child. Although these figures indicate the adult daughters are 50% more likely to emotionally rather than physically abuse a child, the sample is too small for this difference to be highly significant, except as an important pointer toward the need for more research: when almost all of the daughters (90%) reported emotional abuse as a part of the sexually abusive experiences with their mothers, why do so few of them report that they have engaged in emotional abuse of children? There is tremendous prevention potential in answering this question and similar ones regarding relatively low self-reported rates of adult abused daughters sexually or physically abusing children.

Fifteen percent (15%) of the daughters reported that they had *sexually* abused others in childhood. The rate drops to 3% when the daughters refer to their adult sexual abuse of children. Their reported rate of sexually abusing other adults is 7%.

The data may represent insight, self-control, or possibly distancing from children. These daughters, as a group, do not seem overwhelmingly predisposed to engage in high levels of physical, emotional or sexual abuse of children, despite the abuse they suffered themselves. This report by the survivors contradicts the notion that adult survivors of abuse often go on to abuse others.

One of the most difficult questions to answer has been how many people who have been abused go on to become abusers. This problem has been approached in two ways: by studying how many known abusers were victims of sexual abuse in their childhoods; and by looking at how many victim/survivors disclose perpetration of sexual abuse against others. Among the small sample of young female offenders in one study

(Mathews et al., 1989), a 100% victimization history was reported. A survey of 22 inpatient sexual abuse *victim* treatment programs found a rate of 14% of survivor patients disclosing past or present sexual offending behaviors (Bear, 1993); the gender breakdown of the treated survivor population as a whole was 78% females, 22% males. Schwartz (1991) reported that 33% of females presenting with sexual trauma had sexually offended against children. The answer to this question has strong implications for prevention and deserves more study.

The level of continued abuse may decrease in this sample because 90% of the respondents have been in psychotherapy, although many respondents report that they feel they received little help there. Clearly, abuse survivors deserve to be seen as individuals and judged for their own conduct and not stereotyped as a large, amorphous group in which all members are dangerous to children. On the other hand, like everyone else, they are accountable for their behavior.

Regarding other kinds of acting out behaviors, 16% of the survivors reported they frequently engaged in childhood fighting. One area this finding suggests for more exploration is whether women who are charged with physically aggressive and violent crimes were abused in childhood by their mothers.

Thirteen percent (13%) of the respondents to the survey reported delinquent behavior in childhood. Twenty-three percent (23%) of the daughters reported adult stealing, and 29% reported adult lying.

> [I] stole as a child.

> [I] made up big lies about [my] wonderful family life, stole, set fires, etc.

Most children test the potential consequences of lying and stealing, but some of these daughters lied to create an illusion of normal family life.

> At times [I've lied] about the abuse and my feelings. I don't want others to know how bad it was.

One daughter reported that she would say whatever she felt people wanted to hear.

Some abused children engage in risky behaviors, as reflected in this daughter's comments:

> I used to take lots of risks. Now I don't take any. I used to walk across train trestles over water and I can't swim. Be out way after dark. Jumping off garage roofs, etc.

Escaping the Pain: Running Away

Twenty-eight percent (28%) of the daughters ran away during childhood, taking some action to either indicate or escape the pain of the abusive situation they had endured. Running away may have been a consequence of alienation from the mother and others in the family. Although nearly one third ran away, very few told anyone the reason for twenty years or more. For some daughters, running away may not have been a positive coping strategy, but the study did not attempt to correlate running away with its possible negative consequences, such as revictimization, prostitution, drug and alcohol abuse, return to the family by authorities in disgrace, and so on.

UNDER THE SKIN: PHYSICAL CONSEQUENCES OF EMOTIONAL HARM

The survey also asked about physical issues related to the daughters' sexual abuse experiences, and the results were evaluated in extensive consultation with Angela Hoogterp D.O., an osteopath and general psychiatrist. Some of the reported physical symptoms may indicate specific emotional and psychological conditions, including stress. Others may be related to physical aspects of the abuse. Self-neglect or excessive focus on health may stem from the daughters' abusive experiences in their childhoods. For example:

> [I] have a skin disorder that flares up every time I deal with this or in the past when I would see my mother.

Mother/daughter sexual abuse frequently involves physical focus by the mother beyond that expected in normal child care. In most families, mothers monitor the children's health, seek medical attention, and care for sick children. This role allows, even fosters, intense focus on a child's body. Medical professionals often rely heavily on mothers in assessing children's health related needs.

> [You] should have asked if [respondents had] ever been to a doctor for a physical. [My] mother answered all questions and the doctor never looked at me. To him I looked fine on the outside.

In contrast, any early distortion of physical needs may lead some daughters to minimize their own body focus because they do not want to call anyone's attention to their bodies.

Some mothers' attention was stressful, even frightening. These mothers often used the caretaker role for sexual, seductive, or physically dominating activities.

Sexual behavior often is masked by motherly explanations and rationalizations, and thus goes unidentified, which magnifies the rage. HOW the contact was initiated is critical, at least for me. My mother had "medical reasons" for what she did — she pretended to be concerned about my health. Most vividly I remember her prying open my thighs and smearing something on my vagina, to "clean me out."

My mother used her cover as a nurse:
— she told me "they" were considering removing my breast soon after the onset of puberty
— she was obsessed with nonexistent vaginal infections
— she made me take tranquilizers when I was 10 or 11 because "you can't keep crying like that"
— she made frequent anal inspections for worms.

Some daughters report that their mothers' distortions about their bodies or lack of health care was confusing or dangerous.

I almost died of spinal meningitis when I was seven. She had ignored my symptoms because she always thought I was a hypochondriac.

I used to get vaginal infections from the male abuse (father and brother). I told her it felt like I had stickers in my pants. She examined my genitals, found no stickers, and never got me treatment. Once she kept touching my clitoris and I said that it felt good. She slapped me and sent me to my room.

Some daughters are now aware that the abuse made them unable to comfortably focus on their bodies.

Mostly as a child I NEVER got sick because I was so disconnected from my body.

This problem can become an important issue in the daughters' later health care management.

Being unable to recognize my own needs and absolutely terrified to lean on someone else for emotional support or physical support if I'm sick.

I've been unable to take care of my body and became so debilitated with viral/chronic fatigue syndrome I've been unable to work. (I'm) unable to cope with stress — just absorb it until I collapse physically.

For 63% of the respondents, their abuse experiences with their mothers make it difficult to receive certain kinds of medical and dental care.

I thought I was alone in this, too!

❏

Extreme dental problems. Many teeth abscessed before I felt any pain of earlier phase decay.

Some professional women abused by their mothers report not seeing a dentist or having a pelvic exam for 10 to 15 years.

I have been O.K. until now but I have put off going to the doctor for two years.

❏

[I have difficulty with] most [medical care] if it involves undressing or anything more threatening.

❏

Terrified of any medication or substance that causes CNS [Central Nervous System] symptoms (elevated or depressed mood, sedation, etc.). [I was] given tranquilizers (Thorazine, Sinequan) as a child to treat my "nervous stomach aches."

Physical Symptoms of Pain

The respondents in this survey reported pain symptoms, primarily involving headaches and back pain, which, coupled with their avoidance of medical treatment, suggests lives of chronic suffering. Of the respondents, 41% reported having headaches in childhood (compared to 43% reporting adult headaches), and 33% reported having migraine headaches in childhood (compared to 28% with migraines in adulthood).

Respondents reported that 22% experienced back pain in childhood, and 20% of them report back pain as adults. Seven percent (7%) report joint pain (e.g., rheumatoid arthritis) as adults.

Joint pain can cause depression, and low back pain in adults is often a symptom of or caused by depression. Because these data on back pain are consistent, it's difficult to tell exactly what they mean; it may simply reflect a group with bad backs. However, the survey question referred to back pain as related to their sexual abuse by their mothers and should also be considered in that light.

> At times I still feel feverish and ache all over in response to reliving [the abusive] events. I was hospitalized for a year of chronic, low fever prior to the abuse stopping. No cause was found. My legs ached at times and still do after a flashback.

Cardiopulmonary Symptoms

Anxiety often produces disturbances with breathing and heart functions but the cause can also be purely physical. Forty-five percent (45%) of respondents reported childhood shortness of breath when not exerting themselves. Shortness of breath can be caused by a poor physical condition and some diseases such as asthma. However, in my clinical experience I have seen abused clients numbing their bodies by constricting their breathing as a primary defense against distressful emotions.

Thirty-eight percent (38%) of those responding report experiencing childhood palpitations (heart pounding/racing). If there is no physical cause for palpitations, the cause may be anxiety. In addition, adult high blood pressure was cited by 12% of respondents. This condition occurs when the pressure in the arteries does not decrease as the heart relaxes between beats. However, it can also result from stress and anxiety, along with other physical conditions, medications, drugs, or alcohol. When physical causes of elevated blood pressure are ruled out and any needed medications are used, but blood pressure remains high, lifestyle changes and stress reduction may be needed. Such changes may include therapy for childhood trauma.

Digestive Disturbances

In addition to the pain symptoms already mentioned, many respondents report that they experienced other physical problems, including digestive disturbances, such as nausea, vomiting, abdominal pain, constipation, irritable bowel, diarrhea, and ulcers. In general, the respondents reported childhood rates of these symptoms that were remarkably consistent with their reported adulthood occurrence.

> When I read, write, talk or even think about the abuse, I get really bad stomach cramps as though some unconscious part of me were punishing me.

It is worth noting that while many of these symptoms may be caused by a number of medical or physical conditions, they are also stress-related. In addition, there may be a correlation for some of these digestive symptoms with the repeated use of enemas as an instrument of abuse.

In regard to ulcers, 13% of the daughters reported childhood ulcers, while 15% of adult respondents reported them.

Childhood rectal bleeding is not strictly a digestive symptom, but may be related to trauma from enemas or from other objects inserted into the anus. Of the 93 daughters, 11% reported rectal bleeding in childhood. There may be a wide range of causes for the bleeding, including hemorrhoids and cancers. However, the question sought information about *bleeding that they believe connected to the sexual abuse by their mothers*, and that qualification should not be dismissed.

Reproductive and Urinary Symptoms

Female anatomy provides many openings and contact points that make little girls' bodies vulnerable to a wide range of sexual abuse activities. Respondents report problems in reproductive health, such as those listed by one respondent below. The problems have a wide range of causes: medical complications, emotional body distortions, discomfort with female body functions, and the emotions caused by hormonal shifts and reproductive potential. Some pelvic pain is emotional in nature but physical in experience. However, such pain must be investigated until other causes are ruled out. Some daughters report they are numb to sensation in their vaginal and abdominal areas, or they automatically discount pain there as "normal," or they avoid medical exams and treatment, creating the potential for serious problems.

> [I have] reproductive problems! Dysmenorrhea, amenorrhea, rectal problems, breast problems (galactorrhea), denial of my femininity, hatred of my body — particularly in the pelvic area, wanting to be slim and "asexual," polycystic ovaries, pelvic inflammatory disease, and an all around lousy immune system.

That an adult daughter would connect her adult vaginal or bladder infections to her childhood sexual abuse might seem strange, but not if we recognize that the accompanying discomfort is experienced in the same body tissues as the earlier abuse. In addition, such infections require exposure of and attention to these often-numbed body areas.

> I draw the line here and cannot allow anyone to watch [me urinate]. I used to not defecate in women's restrooms in the privacy of my own stall when someone else was in the restroom.

During childhood, this last daughter was made to watch her mother urinate. She now cannot tolerate engaging in any behaviors resembling that original situation.

Conversion or Pseudo-Neurological Symptoms

To greatly simplify, conversion symptoms are emotional stress responses seen or experienced in a physical form (see APA, 1994, p. 452-457 for a detailed discussion of possible causes and symptoms). Among them might be difficulty swallowing for no clear medical reason, non-neurological paralysis, or non-physically based seizures. Our language is rife with examples of these connections. We have all, for example, heard the saying, "I'm having a hard time swallowing that" to mean emotional difficulty with something we don't believe or something painful to accept. Some respondents (9% to 20%) did report difficulties with their throats (sore or "tight" throats in childhood and sore throats in adulthood) related to the abuse. Constriction of the throat is often a symptom of anxiety or depression and has been seen in clinical contexts as potentially connected to the client's holding in emotions and/or not speaking of certain things.

One daughter reported dizziness when she became anxious.

Problems or symptoms mentioned by respondents that might be regarded as conversion symptoms include: loss of voice, speech or hearing impairments, body movement constrictions, urinary retention or difficulty urinating, and tics (sudden, rapid, recurrent, nonrhythmic, stereotyped motor movements; see APA, 1994, p. 100). They commented:

> Body tension is affecting my ability to sing.

> [I had a] sudden, prolonged speech problem of unknown origin and went back into therapy.

My hearing gets slow and reverberates. It's noticeable with music.

[I'm] unable to move or talk [at times].

[I have] a facial tic when stressed or when attempting to recall the incest.

These and many other physical phenomena are considered conversion or pseudo-neurological symptoms when there is no obvious physical reason for them. If trauma survivors explore their odd behaviors and conversion symptoms, they may find new, deeper understandings.

Surgeries

Fourteen percent (14%) of the respondent daughters reported that they had undergone surgeries they felt were related to the incest by their mothers. Some of the daughters had multiple surgeries on their reproductive organs and bladders.

I question whether a hernia which I had surgery on at age 9 was caused by the abuse.

Urethra tube damaged and still undergoing repair procedures to try to undo the damage of scarring and tearing. Also hysterectomy, removal of ovaries and bladder repair.

One daughter reported that she had found a lump in her breast just a month after becoming aware of being sexually abused by her mother in childhood. As I've traveled in several different parts of the country to present information about sexual abuse by mothers, I have met several nurses who work in pre- or post-operative medical settings. These nurses have asked me to address a curious phenomenon: the connection between mother-perpetrated sexual abuse of daughters during the daughters' childhood and later breast and/or uterine cancer. After this happened several times, I became concerned. Several of these nurses told me similar stories about patients desperate to tell someone about childhood sexual abuse just before such surgeries. This issue should be researched and either discounted or addressed properly.

NO REST FOR THE WARY:
SLEEP-RELATED SYMPTOMS

The daughters answered several questions related to sleep and night-time disturbances. No one has greater or more hidden access to children than mothers during the night while others in the household are asleep. As a result, the sexual offending may be associated with sleep. Sleep and darkness may become triggers for fears and flashbacks.

Some daughters may suffer lifelong sleep deprivation that they experience as normal sleep patterns, but which may have a significant impact on mental and physical health. Sleep disturbances are often one reason for entering psychotherapy.

Common disturbances they report fall into four categories: 1) special requirements for safety or sleep; 2) sleep-related fears; 3) disturbed sleep; and 4) intense or disturbing dreams.

Special Requirements

These needs are usually attempts to be safe while sleeping, including conditions that must be present in order for the individual to sleep. When these special conditions cannot be met or are absent, sleep will probably be disrupted or prevented.

Forty-three percent (43%) of the sexually abused daughters report they were unable to sleep without specific clothes on during childhood, declining to 36% in adulthood. These needs are often very specific, as one respondent explained:

> [During childhood I] had to sleep with a pillow held tightly between my legs. Now it's a piece of cloth — a hankie. But I still need it.

Often, the person must have the body covered in certain ways with clothing during sleep, but this can vary with individuals:

> [I'm] unable to sleep in nightgowns or pajamas or any sleepwear. Basically I have three "safe" modes of dress:
> — all my clothes on
> — bra and panties on
> — nude.

Factors affecting this type of variation may include the degree of vulnerability the survivor felt at a given time and the current circumstances. Some survivors experienced changes in their safety requirements for sleep when they moved out of their family homes.

As <u>soon</u> as I had my own place. I loved [nudity]!

The most common need I've heard from abused daughters is the need to sleep in underwear or with some covering of the genitalia. A variation of this problem is great discomfort with exposure during medical exams or surgical procedures.

I ALWAYS had to be covered in bed no matter how hot it was.

Thirty-eight percent (38%) of the daughters responding report that as children they could not sleep without bedding or comfort objects arranged in specific ways.

[I had to have] the bedding tucked in around my shoulders.

I have to have the bedding tucked in at the bottom of the bed. I've tried several times to see if I can go without it but I can't. I feel too vulnerable.

Some daughters reported a need that could be called fortressing:

I used to have to build a fortress of pillows and stuff around and on top of me.

[I] wanted all my stuffed animals around me to protect me and so there wouldn't be any room for her [in the bed] but it didn't work.

Thirty percent (30%) of the respondents reported problems with sleeping in their own beds or said they had trouble sleeping away from home, but this dropped to 16% during adulthood. This insomnia is related to fear for many daughters. Some spent their childhood nights prepared for escape or battle, and some wrote that once they've been awakened, they can't go back to sleep in their own beds.

[I] slept under my bed and slept with a weapon.

I used to sleep in jeans and a shirt on the floor.

[I] need to sleep on the floor or on the couch in the living room to get back to sleep in the middle of the night.

Eleven percent (11%) of the respondents report that even in adulthood they are unable to sleep unless the door is locked. On the other hand, an unlocked door may represent escape, as suggested by one respondent:

I'm more afraid if the door is locked.

Sleep-Related Fears

[I] was afraid I'd "die" if I went to sleep.

Keep in mind that the sleep disturbances are being reported by the respondents within the context of the sexual abuse by their mothers. The following two statements illustrate the source of many fears.

[I had] fear of the crack of light under my bedroom door. As long as that light was on, she was still awake and I was not safe.

[I] always wanted the door "cracked" [partially open] so I could know when she was coming to get me and [I] wouldn't be snuck up on.

Forty-seven percent (47%) of the abused daughters report childhood fear of darkness.

[I had] terror of the dark and of being alone in the house.

[I] sleep with the lights on a lot.

Sleep can be a mystery for children; they may wonder where they "go" and what happens while they are "gone," or unconscious of their surroundings. They may fear this lack of awareness and resist it.

[I had] fear of getting into bed. I thought a man and a woman lived under there, waiting to grab me if I went near the bed. For years I used to get into bed by taking a flying leap from the doorway.

At the time of the incest [by mother and alcoholic uncle] I used to lie awake for hours in terror so great that I'd try to scream, but no sound would come out. I was terrified the man and the woman would reach up and grab me if I got too careless and went anywhere near the edge of the bed.

Several daughters wrote comments about fearing the edge of the bed and of "hanging on" to keep from falling out of bed. "Fear of the edge" may be a symbolic fear of annihilation.

Forty-two percent (42%) of the daughters feared being touched while asleep when they were children, as do 40% as adults.

> I was uncomfortable being touched while sleeping even during "sleepovers" with girlfriends and a cousin. If they touched me, even if they were asleep, I couldn't sleep. I hugged my edge of the bed.

If touched during sleep, the survivors report having panicked, agitated, or even violent responses. These reactions are sometimes true even in long-term relationships where the touch of a partner is very familiar.

> During the first year of marriage I had a very difficult time adjusting to sharing what had been my bed in my apartment. There was a great deal of sleep walking, talking, and "night terrors." I even awoke my husband — beating him and even his head.

> Severe startle response at times in certain stages of sleep if my husband moves. It really wakes him up.

Some "edge hugging" may be to avoid touching anyone else in the bed.

> I still have to sleep on my stomach even if it hurts my back. I cannot tolerate someone else wrapping around me; my vulnerable front feels intolerably exposed.

> [I am] unable to sleep in the same bed with someone else or to fall asleep in the presence of another person.

Sleep Disturbances

Some forms of sleep disturbance can be deeply ingrained. Hyperarousal and sleep disturbances are cited as symptoms of Post Traumatic Stress Disorder (see American Psychiatric Association, 1994, pp. 424 – 429 for a description of PTSD and its symptoms) and can intensify during periods of stress. Sleep disturbances can exacerbate some substance abuse problems.

> [I had an] unpleasant feeling [upon] awakening.

A few daughters in childhood felt uneasy after sleep. Mothers are often involved in putting young children down for naps and into bed at night. They may associate falling asleep with their mothers' power to enforce rules or wishes, as one noted:

We used to have major battles about sleep even when I was very young. If she tried to physically confine me or force me to sleep I would fight her until I was exhausted and when I woke up I would feel tricked and betrayed by my body. I would be awakened by her abusing me during sleep from the time I can remember and I hated sleep.

The respondents cited several specific sleep disturbances, including difficulties with hypnogogic states (the half-awake and half-asleep period), insomnia, sleeptalking, sleepwalking or falling out of bed, extreme tension or rigidity during sleep, and enuresis.

INSOMNIA

Forty-two percent (42%) of the respondents reported insomnia during childhood. This high rate of difficulty sleeping may be due to their reported high levels of anxiety, hypervigilance and depression, making them restless and uneasy. Many of the daughters actually were more vulnerable at bedtime. As little girls, many were afraid of the person who checked their covers, gave them medicine, or who may have "examined" their genitals or "inspected" their rectums "for worms," for example. Some dreaded being told by their mothers to "sleep with me tonight." Such sleeping problems and concerns may persist after the abuse ends.

[I had to] chant to fall asleep to keep [my] mind off the "black hole" which represented the incest before I remembered it. Later, [I] <u>had</u> to listen to a radio to fall asleep and keep [my] mind off the black hole and [to] quiet [my feelings].

Some daughters established rituals or protective systems to fall asleep.

My sister and I had a signal to wake each other up and turn on the light if one of us was scared or had a bad dream. I couldn't sleep without her there.

SLEEPTALKING

Forty percent (40%) of the daughters report that they talked in their sleep as children, and 37% of them report adult sleeptalking. Some children talk in their sleep when overstimulated or stressed.

[I had] nightmares and fear that others will hear me during the nightmares like neighbors or while sleeping at others' homes.

⌐

[I had a] fear of sleeping away from home and waking others with my nightmares. I would often cry or scream out with these nightmares.

SLEEPWALKING

Some respondents noted falling out of bed in childhood (20%) and as an adult (7%). Childhood sleepwalking is reported by 20% of respondents, and 11% report adult sleepwalking. The daughters who fell from bed report they were agitated sleepers and that others often found it difficult to sleep with them. They were given labels like "the thrashing machine," and their behavior while sleeping was often more agitated during times of increased stress.

[I still] fall out if I'm made to sleep in a bed.

The APA reports that sleepwalking is rare in adults and estimates that while between 10% and 30% of children have at least one episode of sleep-walking, only 1% to 5% of all children sleepwalk repeatedly and experience impairment or distress about it at some time during their lives (APA, 1994, p. 589).

[I had] fear of sleepwalking and murdering my mother and father.

Imagine the emotional burden this daughter must have carried to develop such fear and rage.

RIGIDITY

The sleep of some daughters was very constricted and rigid. Some slept virtually without moving, muscles tense.

[I had] light sleep, [and had to] sleep in one spot — not moving, afraid of doing something bad or inappropriate in my sleep.

When there is no medical reason for teeth-clenching and grinding, it is often an indicator of stress and can lead to aching jaw muscles and teeth.

Still clench my teeth/jaws while sleeping. [It] was so bad I had T.M.J. [Temporo-Mandibular Joint] disorder with resulting oral surgery.

ENURESIS

Still another kind of sleep disturbance reported by the daughters involved enuresis, or bedwetting. Twenty percent (20%) of the daughters reported childhood bedwetting which continued into adulthood for 7%. Some daughters also reported daytime incontinence in both childhood and adulthood. While both adult and childhood enuresis can be a symptom of medical conditions such as diabetes, the cause may also be emotional (see APA, 1994, pp. 108–110).

> As a child and as an adult I can't sleep without underpants on. If I do [sleep without them] I not only am very anxious and have a hard time getting to sleep, but it's very likely that I will start to wet the bed before I wake up. I think my old trick of withdrawing feeling from my genitals is at least partially responsible.

The APA (1994, p. 109) reports the following data on bedwetting: 1) at age 5, it appears in 3% of girls; 2) it appears in 2% of girls at age 10; and 3) it is almost nonexistent in girls by age 18.

The causes of bedwetting are complex, but the findings from this study are stunning compared to the APA findings among girls in general. If we assume the bedwetting reported during childhood was primarily before age 5, then these daughters had a bedwetting rate nearly 7 times the norm for little girls. However, bedwetting and daytime incontinence was often experienced much later in childhood and into adolescence than is normal.

The reported adult rate of bedwetting among these respondents is *more than twice* that for girls aged 5 and under. This experience can be embarrassing and humiliating, possibly a significant element in the fact that only one daughter commented in writing on bedwetting and incontinence in addition to providing requested data. It's damaging to self-esteem to be a grown woman without full bladder control. This problem may worsen or re-emerge during periods of stress or when new memories or aspects of the abuse emerge.

UNRESTFUL SLEEP

The chances of disturbed sleep are very high when children sleep with their perpetrators. They may get little true rest and expend tremendous energy trying to stay safe, decrease physical contact, and contain their emotions. Two respondents described childhood and adult effects:

> I pretended to be asleep while I frantically tried to figure out what to do. Then I'd roll over "in my sleep" so she couldn't reach me. I was a real restless sleeper.

> I slept in her bed for what now seems like an eternity. Deducing from other events in my life it was about a year. Since remembering and knowing that [I was] abused many of [these sleep problems] have appeared and/or increased in frequency and intensity.

Only one (1.07%) of the 93 daughters reported no childhood or adult sleep disturbances. She was severely abused by a psychotic mother until age 2 or 3, when her grandparents intervened. Her mother was so severely mentally ill that the rest of her family did not attempt to cover it up. Perhaps she had less to wonder about and fewer fears to disrupt her sleep. She grew up separated and/or protected from her mother's behaviors and says simply:

> I think I slept well.

To Sleep Perchance to Dream: Nightmares, Terrors and Dreams

Sixty-two percent (62%) of the ninety-three respondents reported childhood nightmares in which the dream is remembered upon awakening. All children can have frightening dreams, but the nightmares reported by the daughters frequently focus on their mothers as the frightening element. Night terrors (sudden awakening accompanied by extreme agitation and lack of awareness of its cause) were reported, and they decreased as the daughters resolved abuse issues.

The reported nightmares sometimes held images of death, mutilation, destruction of their bodies, of being trapped or frozen stiff, as well as of being sexually threatened and abused. The night terrors and nightmares seemed to decrease in adulthood but for some daughters reappeared when they were under stress, became conscious of new memories or aware of the abuse for the first time, or were experiencing situations with similar emotional content to the earlier trauma(s).

To put these reports into context, the APA (1994, p. 581) reports that nightmares "of sufficient intensity to disturb their parents" occur in about 10% to 50% of children aged 3 to 5 years and that as many as 50% of the adult population has had at least one nightmare. "Night terrors" are called "sleep terrors" by the APA (1994, pp. 583–587), and when the episodes are repeated and distressing, they amount to "Sleep Terror Disorder." Episodes (as opposed to the disorder) typically occur in 1% to 6% of children and in less than 1% of adults.

Given the unlimited access the mothers had to these child victims, dreams may have been a safe form of tension release for the children who probably had to hide their feelings from their mothers. By turning reality into symbols, the child maximizes the concealment; the emotional impact of the dreams is often present while the meaning and reality is hidden. This transformation of reality allows the child to cope with her reality as though it were a frightening movie. Children can re-experience the reality and per-haps the emotions but they don't really understand or relate to it.

DREAMING ON AND ON

Fifty-eight percent (58%) of the respondents reported recurrent dreams in childhood. Sometimes these dreams go into a remission of sorts, only to re-emerge and compel the adult daughter to seek treatment. Recurring dreams can be very unsettling because the individual has no control over their occurrence.

> I had a recurrent dream throughout early childhood and into adolescence of living between the floors in the house where [I grew up]. [In the dream] I used a separate entrance and could see into the main parts of the house [as it actually did exist], but I didn't know how to get there. My father, mother and an older brother lived in the main part of the house.

These dreams may contain incomprehensible or coded information. Their meaning may be resisted or denied, so they repeatedly return, demanding, so to speak, to be understood. By storing memory in repeated dreams, a daughter puts reality aside or changes it into an unrecognizable form, but it still has enough power to cause an emotional discharge when it reappears.

Later the dream's symbolism, if any, may be understood and the dreamer is often amazed that she couldn't (or wouldn't) see its meaning.

This process is reflected by the respondent who dreamed of living between floors:

> It still amazes me that for the first 9 years after I'd dealt with the sexual abuse by my brother and father, that I managed to repress the sexual abuse by my mother. It was years before I looked back and remembered that she'd been in that dream, too.

The symbolism of some repeated dreams is intriguing, as in the following one from a daughter whose mother was mentally ill.

> [I've had a] recurrent dream since childhood of my mother with her legs chopped off at the knees and she's holding herself up in a standing position acting as if nothing is wrong.

Such dreams may seem benign when recalled by adult women. When explored more deeply, however, they may cause discomfort and agitation. The dream's images and symbolism are often profoundly powerful. Having first appeared in childhood, these dreams may repeat in striking detail even when the individual is 20 to 40 years old.

NEW DREAMS

Some dreams seem new to the dreamer. The daughter may have dreamed it before but cannot bring that to her conscious attention. New dreams may be a sign that psychotherapy is going well for a client, and sometimes a "new" dream is the reason for seeking treatment.

I've found there are often two types of new dreams among daughters sexually abused by their mothers. The-past-and-people-revisited dreams symbolize the daughter returning to her past. They may return in the dream to the house, land or town where she grew up, the old neighborhood or school, or something else that symbolizes her past and childhood. People forgotten for years may be in these dreams. After such dreams are explored, clients often begin to see old situations in new ways, or they may evoke changed or added emotions or perceptions.

The past-revisited dreams may occur while new and deeper individuation is occurring. For example, here is a new dream from the daughter whose mother's legs were chopped off in a recurrent dream:

> I've had dreams in recent months as I've worked on this [the abuse] of my mother acting as a "childlike seductress" towards me and I get so angry. In one dream, however, I calmly asked her, "Who taught you that?" I asked

her a couple more times and she stopped the behavior and said a male
name I did not recognize.

This dream is rich with roles, metaphors, actions, and questions. Compare it to her recurrent dream in which her mother was ignoring the distortion of her own body. In the new dream, this daughter is empowered and does not accept the previous status quo.

Multiple revisitations to the same scene or person seem to be searches for answers or needed insight or to see if anything has changed. Sometimes these dreams are "Will you please look at this?" messages.

One daughter in this study dreamed she revisited her childhood home and from the street saw her family calmly eating a meal while the house burned. She then looked into the house next door and saw her alcoholic ex-husband's house on fire. Finally she saw that the next house on this street was her lover's home, and it too was on fire. She crossed the street to a house where she now lived and sat on the porch while the fire department came. None of the occupants voluntarily left their burning houses. In real life, none of those individuals dealt with reality very well.

Clearly, sleep disturbances and dreams among the daughters of abusive mothers is an issue that deserves more study:

I think you are right to [focus on] the role of dreams in the healing process.
They have been enormously powerful for me.

KEEP HOPE ALIVE: OBSERVATIONS OF THE PAST, NOT DESTINIES FOR THE FUTURE

The daughters' responses reported here paint a fairly depressing picture of the future for young girls who are being or recently have been sexually abused by their mothers. Keep in mind, however, that the women in this study were abused at a time when there were few if any resources and almost no help, a situation that is changing, albeit too slowly. Are these daughters doomed to lives of sadness and ill health? No. The following daughter, advocating for others like herself, gives good advice and encouragement:

Try anything that works. While I have not integrated into my body, I
exercise daily (swimming is the best for making my body feel okay). I have

had regular massages (frightening but I need to know all touch isn't sexual) and I see a chiropractor occasionally to get out the inevitable physical distortions caused by the stress of dealing with this.

The combination of elements that lead to good emotional and physical health will vary with each daughter. I encourage my clients and other survivors to explore their own bodies and healthier ways of being. I strongly support their demands for competence and compassion from their physical and mental health care providers. I urge us to support each other in this quest. I encourage us to not only learn to love ourselves more than we have, but also to accept our bodies and enjoy them.

Part Six

CONFRONTATION, RESOLUTION, AND SEPARATION

CHAPTER 13

Adult Survivors' Relationships with Their Mothers

As might be expected, there are often disturbing breakdowns in relationships between these daughters and their mothers stemming from the abuse. The daughters are left to struggle with emotions and needs in the aftermath of their early abusive experiences. According to the reports of the daughters, some of the relationships evolved — and some ended — in various ways.

EMOTIONS TO CONFRONT: ANGER

Anger and hostility are common in mother-daughter relationships where there has been abuse, as we discussed in Chapter 12. The daughters often suppress any anger because they feel social pressure to maintain a relationship with their mothers.

> You may get a lot of messages (from society, family, therapist, etc.) to either forgive or forget — after all, "She's your mother."

Until resolution comes from within, however, the pain and anger are real and reasonable. Not all daughters continue to carry rage at their mothers; some resolve such feelings under the influence of social norms.

FEELING WITH THE BODY: TOUCH

Touch is often more profound and powerful than words. Eighty-two (82%) percent of the daughters report that even as adults they are not comfortable with being touched by their mothers. In answer to the survey question, one wrote:

> DEFINITELY not.

Touch is the most fundamental and powerful form of human communication and an integral part of mother-child relationships. However, these daughters may experience their mothers' touch as a trigger for painful memories. At the same time, their mothers' touch may be desperately desired and actively sought. One respondent sent in a poem to relate how complex the topic of touch can be with an abusive mother:

I steel myself
    for her touch
Her cheek accidentally
    brushes mine as she
    stiffly
offers an obligatory hug.
My insides scream NO
and I hear the child I once was
    warning me it's not safe!
Don't believe! Run. Hide. Go.
But I'm an adult now.
She has no power anymore.

I take my inside child tightly
by the hand. I press her small
hand to my heart, look into
her eyes and promise her that
I will never let
    anyone
hurt her like that again.
Her bottom lip trembles and is
    reflected in my own.
The child and I are intertwined
and like a two-tone ball rolling
down a hill I'm alternately
child, adult, child, adult.

There may have been very little safe and caring touch in these relationships which the daughters experienced as normal and nurturing. Even accidental touch could be disturbing:

> I couldn't understand my feelings of repulsion and nausea sometimes when my mother would hug me. Having her live with me again — even for a few months — has been the catalyst of my remembering.

> I have gone through periods where being touched [by her] brought on panic. [But I can now touch her] as though I could heal her or comfort her, as though [it were] evidence that I love her or accept her.

Sixty-five percent (65%) of the survivors reported that violence accompanied the sexual abuse, which may be a major factor in the daughters' intolerance of their mothers' touch. Eighty-one percent (81%) of these daughters report they are uncomfortable touching their mothers.

> She stopped touching me at age two. I didn't touch her — she was like a cold stone.

The survey did not ask if the daughters had a hunger for human touch, but some reported that it is a problem:

> I feel [an] extremely intense need to be touched, held.

Some daughters have a deep longing for safe, non-sexual touch.

> The thing that she [my inner child] most wants to hide is the feeling that she would like to be safely held. That has never been enough for other people. They have always tied that desire [for holding] to sexual activity and she is not ready for that. She needs to know that she can be loved in something other than a sexual way. She needs to know that there are some people who will not run screaming if she becomes emotional. She needs to learn how to speak.

Ninety-three percent (93%) of the daughters report they have felt as if they were emotionally and/or physically "frozen" when touched. Some commented in detail:

> [I have a] fear of being touched and "freezing" when being touched.

> Maybe I feel "frozen" sometimes when someone touches me. [I] just feel very isolated and unfeeling — as if I'm being used.

This feeling of being immobilized may occur in sexual and medical situations or may trigger flashbacks or panic reactions, as noted by two respondents:

223

[I have a] fear of being touched — especially when crying or angry.

Before therapy, almost always [felt frozen], if [touched] by a woman.

Touch by the mothers or others may cause the daughters to feel flooded with emotions. Their reactions maybe a mixture of "power outage" (feeling immobilized) and of being flooded with too much energy at the same time. This reaction is usually beyond the survivor's control.

The sexual abuse may have forced the daughters to numb their bodies in order to tolerate their mothers' touch. This necessity to numb themselves is a problem for children whose mothers continue to touch them as a part of child care. Some may learn to generalize their numbing to their entire body and to all human touch.

Ninety-six percent (96%) of the daughters are aware of discomfort with certain circumstances and people involving touch or specific forms of touch. The specific issues vary widely, but the discomfort is remarkably common among the daughters.

Many daughters carry this discomfort into relationships with their own daughters, something about which they often feel sad and shameful. Fifty-four percent (54%) of the respondents report they are uncomfortable with little girls' bodies. Reluctance to touch little girls may be conscious or unconscious attempts to prevent potential sexual feelings or abuse of children. Some report they are so careful or uncomfortable with touching their own daughters that the lack of touch in their relationship can border on neglect. They may fear not knowing the appropriate boundaries, as one daughter noted:

> It was painful to face that I was not safe with my mother. The most entangled part of me is that I'm not sure where affection stopped and incest began.

Such confusion is painful. They may fear both touching and failure to be an appropriate, physically affectionate mother.

KEEPING QUIET:
CONFRONTING SILENCE ABOUT THE ABUSE

Seventy percent (70%) of the daughters say that as adults they have not tried to talk to their mothers about the sexual abuse. They report that they are unwilling to take the risk and that they realize the chances of a positive outcome may be small. The daughters who *have* tried to communicate with their mothers about the abuse report that denial is their mothers' most common response. Another reported response to the daughters' raising the topic is for the mother or other family members to attack the daughter, as some wrote:

> She totally denied it occurred.

> When I confronted my mother about all this recently she said "I never touched you! You always touched me." So what is that supposed to mean? In her mind she is innocent. In my case I think the abuse was the kind where she made it look like I was the initiator and it was, from my memories, subtle.

> At this point I don't think I ever will [talk to my mother]. Why be abusive to myself? [Question: Has she tried to talk to you?] Are you kidding? She rearranges reality and memory day by day.

> Although I have not been able to talk with my mother about her abuse of me, we have talked about my father's abuse of me, and my mother's and my relationship. She says it's like we didn't have a relationship. I agree. Even the sexual abuse felt like it was from a dissociated, not really present part of her, and not relating to me, but to my body.

Many daughters assume that such exploration with their mothers will lead to more problems. Some mothers seem to seal off all memory of their abusive behaviors.

> I doubt that she remembers it, consciously. She'd deny it anyway and say I'm "crazy." Who needs that?

> I have tried to talk to her of other things like my feelings, my father's alcoholism, my own alcoholism, and she shut me up by saying: "Oh, you and your feelings! If you're going to let your feelings out they're going to get stepped on like a cat's tail. No one wants to hear your feelings!"

Some daughters cannot tolerate their mothers' reactions to raising abuse issues.

> [We've talked about the physical abuse] ... yes. [But] I didn't remember the sexual abuse until after her death. She cried and accused me of not allowing her to forget the past. I shut up.

I just moved in with her to try to get this straightened out but it just made it worse.

According to the daughters' reports an even higher percentage (91%) of the mothers have never tried to talk to their daughters about the sexual abuse. Clearly, the abusive mothers rarely initiate talk about their sexual abuse of their daughters.

I think the general public needs to realize the NO child molester is ever going to actually admit, "Oh yeah, sure, I do that all the time!"

The mothers avoid talking about their abusive behaviors with remarkable success. Some daughters believe their mothers have no conscious memory of it because they were in an altered state of reality at the time of the abuse. Some of these daughters believe their mothers remember but avoid the reality of their actions. No matter the reason for the silence, the results are the same. The daughter must carry the secret to maintain a relationship with her mother and any pretense that the relationship is normal, and in order to believe she is loved like other children.

Ninety-nine percent (99%) of the daughters have not successfully talked with their mother about the sexual abuse.

What is successful? I did talk to her and she denied she did anything wrong.

I know only one daughter who believes she had successfully communicated with her mother about the sexual abuse after intense work with a skilled therapist. But the daughter still does not fully trust her mother and does not allow her to be alone with the grandchildren.

Another daughter's remarkable mother initiated the contact and revealed she had sexually abused the daughter, but the daughter had no conscious memories of her mother's past abusive behaviors. This mother told her daughter because she was concerned about her daughter's serious depression. She and her daughter are working on this together. This cooperation, however, is a rare exception, and I respect this mother for taking such a risk.

My husband sent a letter outlining [the abuse issues] and I sent therapy bills telling them they should accept responsibility. She denied it and said I was crazy and evil. Now there's no contact.

There is often painful silence in these relationships, and at the same time, it is often a vital issue between them.

We will never expose the true extent of sexual abuse by mothers if we wait for the mothers to tell us. We must learn about their abusive behaviors from their adult children.

FORGIVENESS

Forgiving a sexual abuser can be a controversial issue, regardless of the abuser's gender. There may be pressure from family members, other relatives, friends, therapists, religious advisors or internalized religious beliefs, and from the abuser herself for the survivor of sexual abuse to forgive the abuser. Some survivors and therapists (Bass & Davis, 1994; Bear & Dimock, 1988, among others) have questioned whether forgiveness helps survivors to heal, or merely serves to minimize the abuse and its impact and interferes in the survivor's processing of emotions about the abuse and the abuser.

Among this survey's respondents, 47% say forgiving their mothers is difficult, and 33% of the daughters say it is not. Many of these daughters report they have felt pressure from all the usual sources and even from other survivors to forgive their mothers. This pressure can cause unnecessary internal struggle for these daughters.

I'm confused about forgiveness.

[I had] open hostility to people who told me to "forgive" her. [Like my father].

Pressure to forgive may eventually ease for some daughters.

[It's] not [an issue] anymore — but it was for a long time.

Even though a third of the daughters say that forgiving their mothers is not difficult, 75% of the abused daughters say they have not forgiven their mothers for the abuse, while 9% of the respondents say they have. Most of the daughters I've spoken with about forgiveness see it as something that may occur in the future.

No, [it's not an issue for me]. I haven't seriously considered it. That seems down the line to even think about it.

NO, BUT I'M GETTING THERE.

It's too early.

For others, it may be impossible to forgive, as some noted:

> And [I] have no intention to [forgive her].

> I doubt that I'll live long enough. It becomes irrelevant as I work things through.

> IT IS SOMETHING UNFORGIVABLE FOR WHICH THERE IS, IN MY OPINION, NO EXCUSE. THE DECEPTION AND THE MASQUERADE IS EVEN MORE UNFORGIVABLE THAN THE ABUSE.

CLOSENESS AND SEPARATION

Some of the respondent daughters fled their homes; others were ensnared and had difficulties achieving a healthy separation from abusive mothers. Contrary to common opinion, people who have conflicts frequently remain in fierce union despite any appearance of disinterest and disconnection. Thus, even the fiercely independent and clearly "stuck" daughters may remain in emotional union with their mothers, but the union may take different forms. The daughters who seem clearly fettered in the relationship with their mothers are the most recognizable. One wrote:

> Every time I tried to separate from her emotionally, I was in effect damaging myself in some way. I had merged with her completely and when I would assert my independence, I was terrified that something terrible would happen to her — who was I if I wasn't her??

Many grown daughters remain close to their abusive mothers. Confusion, lack of boundaries and inappropriate behaviors may continue, and the fight to disengage can last for years.

> My mom's needs dominated every aspect of my life and she saw me as an extension of her. As an adult, at age 35, I am just beginning to differentiate myself and find my own likes/dislikes and talents. Because my mom told me over and over how wonderful, brilliant and talented I am I have suffered between extreme grandiosity and feeling like sewer scum.

> I find that the steps I take to being healthy, like bonding with friends, forming healthy relationships, making enough money, admitting I want a fun sexual relationship with a man all feel like a betrayal of my mother. I have to work to separate and move on, even though she is dead. Do other people feel this way?

Thirty-seven percent (37%) of the respondents report they currently feel drawn to maintain, re-establish, or create a relationship with their mothers. Forty-seven percent (47%) of them say they do not want such relationships. About half the daughters seem to be moving away from their mothers emotionally.

In answer to another question, 75% of the daughters indicated that they feel the urge to withdraw or separate from their mothers. There may be struggle and ambivalence at the thought of cutting that tie, but the urge is there for many. Some are actively working at withdrawal.

> [I am] mentally and emotionally quite divided on this.

> I am on the edge of withdrawing.

> [I] am successfully abstinent from [my relationship with my mother], one day at a time.

The adult daughters may have to end or greatly restrict their relationship to their mothers for their own lives to move forward. Fortunately for her, the following respondent has resolved many conflicts from the past about her mother and the abuse she suffered.

> I am so grateful to be living now with so many tools of recovery and healing. These things were not so available for our parents.

According to the daughters' reports, some mothers resent and resist healthy individuation and distance by their daughters. Some feel hurt or insulted that they can no longer make their daughters address their needs first.

> [These] mothers may also have poor boundaries between themselves and their daughters, and use their daughters (as less-than-a-whole-person) to meet their own needs, being outraged at any attempts towards SEPARATENESS.

Almost by definition, abusive mothers have a low tolerance or capacity for healthy change, and the daughters are left to determine how such separation occurs. Clinicians with clients in such a position need to support these daughters to cope with conflicting feelings, and most of all, must find a way to keep their own conflicting feelings about mother-daughter separation out of the session. As one daughter wrote:

> The incest survivor has a right to be angry with her mother and to not want to see her or have her in her life.

229

In addition to the often internalized personal pressure to remain in union with the mother, some daughters feel there are also social pressures to not separate very far from their mothers.

> The culture and cultural assumptions encourages women to be like their mothers so [it] hides the fact that incest blurs and hinders female self development. [It is] desirable for women to develop their own selves as persons [e.g. to choose to not be with or like their mothers].

Sixty-three percent (63%) of the respondents say they've been unable to achieve independent adult status in relation to their mothers.

> [I] do not feel alive separated from her.

The daughters may find moving on and away from their mothers and their families of origin difficult, no matter how appropriate the leaving might be.

> What has seemed most devastating to me is the fact that until recently I have felt like a deficient human being because I did not love my parents. My mother encouraged my belief that I was incapable of loving. I spent most of my life pretending feelings because I was terrified that if I stopped pretending I would find out she was right.

TOUCH NOT: PARENTING

Seventy-four percent (74%) of the daughters report their sexual abuse experience has affected their parenting abilities. Only 4% of respondents said it has not. Fifty-four percent (54%) of the respondents say they feel discomfort at times while caring for, touching, or viewing a little girl's body, and they believe their discomfort is connected to their own sexual abuse. Fewer of the daughters responding to the survey (32%) say they're aware of similar discomfort with boys.

Some of these daughters found raising little girls especially difficult. A few were unable to touch their daughters even in infancy. They may struggle with an introjection of their own abusive mothers.

> Feeling afraid of my own children (girls). I don't know if I'm my mother and they are me sometimes. I feel so sorry for them I can hardly STOP myself from begging their forgiveness even though I've been an excellent, kind mother to them. I feel as though my mother is inside me, trying to get out. That because I have been the repository of so much evil, I should probably never be around children even though I never have or would abuse them.

Dilemmas like the one this daughter faces desperately need to be understood by clinicians treating women abused by their mothers. Despite feeling alone and fearful in their pain, the daughters may not become abusive but instead withhold warm, loving gestures and refrain from touching their own children, especially little girls.

What happens to these little granddaughters of abusive mothers? Do they become part of an increasing group of women who feel unloved and abandoned? Can they love and nurture their own children, the abusive mothers' great-grandchildren? Where does society count this cost of mother abuse in its denial that it occurs?

What does it cost the daughters? Some indication can be gained from the woman who wrote of her concern for her daughters but feels her own, abusive mother inside herself:

I'd rather have my skin ripped off than to sit facing a therapist while I talk about this.

Oppressed people come to believe that they have a foreshortened future or limited options. They also frequently believe that they themselves are responsible for their failures and problems. This self-blame is often encouraged and even planted in the oppressed by their oppressors. The oppressed may live in an environment that not only allows oppression but reinforces it as justified. If we are willing to look, we will see these dynamics at work in many of these daughters.

The oppressive dynamics of the daughters' lives may be some of the most devastating consequences of their sexual abuse. Some daughters decide very early in life that they cannot or will not be a parent. For some, it is a conscious decision. For others, it is a vague discomfort or a dreaded thing to be avoided. While parenthood is not necessarily the absolute and ultimate fulfillment of women's destinies, all women should have the right to choose it (or not). The daughters of abusive mothers have real and legitimate concerns about coping with the responsibility of being parents that should be addressed.

What is perhaps most oppressive in this regard is a terrible, often very premature, deeply embedded terror that a sexually abused daughter is forever flawed and should never allow herself to become a mother or have contact with children. On the other hand, some daughters face a horrible dilemma in having a little girl whom they cannot touch and nurture because of their fear. Some daughters may even inadvertently neglect their little girls in an attempt to be better parents than their own abusive mothers.

That dynamic raises the question: to what extent does sexual abuse by mothers become part of a continuing oppressive cycle that foreshortens the futures and limits the options of succeeding generations of women and girls?

ABANDONED OR SET FREE: MOTHER'S DEATH

The death of an abusive mother may be initially disturbing for an abused daughter but later may be a great relief. Sixty-one percent (61%) of the daughters have concerns about their mothers' future death (if living) or report that the death was emotionally traumatic.

Death or potential death of an abusive mother can be emotionally paralyzing and related to enmeshment. The daughters were physically "re-enmeshed" with their mothers after birth through sexual abuse. As young children, the daughters may have been confused about where their bodies left off and their mothers' bodies began. When this confusion is unresolved, the thought of the mother's death may be perceived by the daughter as her own death. These daughters are often deeply involved with their mothers at the time of death.

Some daughters may hope their mothers will die, and some express their harsh feelings bluntly.

> I often think about and fear how I'll feel when my mother dies.

> She has terminal cancer. It's been a real roller coaster for my sisters and me. It feels pretty worked out right now. She feels dead already to me.

> My parents became critically ill and I felt great ambivalence about my role in helping them, dealing with their deaths, etc.

> The sooner the better. (I have money issues.) I feel unable to support myself and have felt like I had to emotionally "whore" for her financial aid. I wish she'd die. I could use the money!

To tell this daughter she really doesn't mean what she says is like poking a bear with a stick. Her feelings are what they are; the job of a therapist is to help such clients to identify and express those feelings in ways that do not cause harm. The daughters may feel great pain when their offending mothers die.

[Her death] was extremely traumatic for me.

My clinical experience indicates that some daughters enter psychotherapy around the time their mothers die. Many of the daughters in this study commented on issues surrounding their feelings regarding the deaths of their abusive mothers.

It was the biggest relief of my life. I realized it almost immediately and expected some guilt to hit me for feeling that way but it's been almost ten years now and that's all it ever was. Just a big relief. I've slept better since then.

[Her death was a] relief to me and yet traumatic in that it triggered depression, memories and pain.

The daughters may feel new emotional freedom following their mothers' deaths; they may now be able to think more freely and fully about their abuse for the first time. On the other hand, as two daughters' comments indicate, this death may also bring them face to face with a long-standing dilemma.

Mom had to die before I could remember it.

Even though you may be deathly afraid of your mother and hate her behavior, you still love her because she is your mom.

The relationship may have been emotionally dead for years for some daughters, so a mother's physical death brings almost no response.

No [it was not traumatic]. I didn't care.

Some readers may be shocked by some of these statements, but they are honest and simply reflect the absence of a need to pretend or to protect social stereotypes.

For other daughters, their mothers' deaths may make forgiveness and resolution possible.

She died several years ago. Just forgive her and move on. The more I forgive her and understand, the more I can allow her memory or "being" to be close to me. It's difficult but worth it.

HOPE FOR HEALING AND RESOLUTION

Seventy-four percent (74%) of the survivors believe the abuse by their mother had such a serious effect on their lives that it was not possible to ever become whoever they could have been without the abuse. In other words, for these daughters, there is no true "recovery," no ability to completely undo the effects, unlearn the negative lessons, recapture innocence and trust. And yet, there is hope. As one daughter commented:

I'm working on it.

In a question aimed at identifying the degree of hope they have for recovery, the respondents were asked if they believe the after effects of the abuse experience are things they will have to manage the rest of their lives; 70% of respondents answered yes, 8% said no, and 21% were unsure.

Given their present levels of pain, struggle and isolation, their belief that there are few good therapy options, along with social denial, these survivors are not very hopeful about recovery.

No cure — but believe [it] can be managed.

It can't be gotten over quickly. It is a _lifelong_ personal management problem.

However, some respondents do believe they will have a full recovery, and we should support and foster that perception.

I feel it's mostly handled now, but I _did_ get very good help. I found loving, maternal people who have nurtured me. Like Inie in _When You're Ready_ but a little different.

[I believe I will struggle with this] a longtime. [But] I'm getting there.

Some of the respondents report an ability to mend and move on:

I am in full recovery.

Each daughter was asked, "All in all, do you feel you have resolved this issue?" and 16% of the daughters answered yes, 82% said no, and 2% of the respondents indicated that they were unsure.

Asked if they believe they can reach a point where their abuse experience does not interfere with their lives in any way, 19% of the respondents said yes, 39% said no, 41% of the daughters answered that they were unsure. Some added comments:

If it ever really ends.

Sometimes I do [think it will be resolved] and sometimes it creeps back up.

One daughter related the story that she was born with a *caul*, or part of the amniotic sack, covering her head. In the tradition of her Irish heritage, being born with a caul was a sign of luck, particularly for sailors, because a person born with a caul would not drown. This excerpt from a poem she wrote indicates her route to resolution as her mother throws herself into metaphorical deep water and resists any help but hers:

And she nearly pulled me under,
strangling me,
clutching me at the throat,
and needing me.
I nearly went with her
but I had to let go.
I will always mourn that moment.
Blood of my blood
Flesh of my flesh
My mother who gave me light of
    day,
I could not choose for you.
In amazement, I am alive.
In awe, I am healing.
In the abyss, I choose to live.

I turned in the current
and with the strength left in me,
swam for the rocky shore.
In gratitude,
I hold the ones who gave me
    breath
'til I could breathe myself,
Who gave me love
'til I could love myself,
Who dragged me from the river
and taught me to live my own life
when I didn't know how.
Born with a caul, I did not drown.
Born with a calling, I have chosen
    to live.

235

CHAPTER 14

Conclusions and Comments

In closing, I want to note a few conclusions I have drawn from conducting this survey. First, if these data and the ideas in this book are discomfiting, I can only say that the findings are as reported, or, the data are the data. Some of it is still discomfiting to me, too.

Second, and perhaps most important, I hope this study spawns new research, raises issues, and creates the need to know more. I make no claim that this is the exact picture of sexual abuse by mothers or its impact on all victims. But based on these findings and the testimony of the many women sexually victimized by their mothers, I have to conclude that women are capable of independent and destructive sexual abuse. Therapy, medical, legal, social work and correctional professionals, citizens and others who do not see it may simply not want to see it. I will not evade the truths that mother-daughter sexual abuse happens, that it is damaging, and that it may be more violent and hidden than anyone except the victims realized.

Third, ignoring this abuse will not make it stop, and society ignores it to our own peril.

Further, this study has raised some specific concerns for me. I am concerned for the wellbeing of some of the survivors of sexual abuse by mothers. The suicide rate and mental and physical health problems are real. The survivors' sense of being disconnected from society profoundly hurts them and their ability to survive: I know that two of the women in this study are now dead from either suicide or self-destructive behaviors stemming from abuse by their mothers. The data on substance abuse, depression, ulcers, and other illnesses raise my level of alarm.

I am also concerned about the wellbeing of the perpetrator mothers. Their mental health problems, substance abuse, and social isolation are also real. I do not excuse their behavior, but I do acknowledge the lack of services available to them in many areas. I have seen fear in the eyes of some mothers who have approached me at conferences where I spoke.

I'm concerned that this form of abuse is still hidden. There may be additional aspects of it still hidden. How will we make it possible for these survivors to have their needs met?

I'm concerned that our society will continue to not want to know about this abuse, will continue to bury its collective head in ignorance, not wanting to give up the old secure but inaccurate mommy myths. Will this information come at a time when society has become desensitized and perhaps even indifferent about abuse victims and their needs?

I'm concerned that society will not take abuse between mothers and daughters seriously because both victim and perpetrator are women. In addition, people might resist this information because they want to continue to stereotype and view women as nurturers incapable of such abuse, as non-sexual protectors, and as somehow morally "better than men."

Most of all, I'm concerned that *every day* there are new, silent child victims who may live lives similar to those reflected in these data.

I think these data challenge us to make some changes in the following areas:

Prevention:

Do the current prevention programs address sexual abuse by females/mothers adequately? How many times have you heard females and/or specifically mothers mentioned in lists or identified in photographs of possible abusers?

Assessment:

Do our current medical, mental-health assessment and criminal investigation protocols for child abuse and neglect address the possibility of female and mother perpetrators and these issues? What will we accept as evidence of a sexual assault by a female?

Treatment:

Do we train our professionals to recognize and treat sexual abuse by females? Do our self-help groups create a climate in which survivors of sexual abuse by mothers can work? Do we develop programs to adequately treat women's and mothers' sex offending? Is there full prosecution of female perpetrators?

We have a long ways to go in many areas. To further expand our resources, a companion volume discussing treatment implications and suggesting treatment approaches and guidelines based on my clinical experience and the responses of the women in the study will (soon, I hope) follow the publication of this work.

I believe we'll need to be ready to give up our adherence to "warm and fuzzy" stereotypes of mothers to really understand and address these concerns. We have to recognize the full spectrum of female sexuality, behavior and emotions.

Conducting this survey and writing up its findings has been a long and difficult task. I wish to thank again the women and men who participated in this study and spoke so eloquently, and I thank all who have helped in any way to bring it to fruition. I've seen incredible growth in many survivors in this study whom I know or have come to know personally. I've felt joyful about the change in some. I recently attended a performance of a daughter who sang with strength and energy. I know of happy marriages, new skills and strengths, successful psychotherapy, new babies, new businesses, and new educational efforts. I feel strongly that these survivors have much to offer, and we must create the conditions in which they can heal and add their energies and strengths.

It is complete.
The dream is real.
Late in the day two women sat on
    a hill
And watched the sun turn
    golden.
They knew the darkness would
    come again.
The coolness. The chill and fear.
But they took this moment to
    reflect.
Finally one said to the other
"Is this true?"
The second pondered quietly until
    her answer was
    ripe.
"Yes."

Later they were joined by their
    brother.
He too said, "Yes.
It is real."
They remained in the stillness for
    awhile.
Together. Quiet.
Feeling the profoundness of their
    shared truth.
They know.
This really happens.
Who will sing with them?
Who will learn this song?
How loud must a song be before
    the sun rises?

Appendix

THE SONS

APPENDIX A

Incest Between
Mothers and Sons

A survey of nine adult sons sexually abused by their mothers is briefly summarized here, with the acknowledgment that it is difficult to compare samples of such disparate sizes. These men were contacted almost exclusively through presentations I gave on mother-daughter sexual abuse. Confirming this sexual abuse of sons is important in and of itself. In addition, many daughters appreciate contact and sharing experiences with these men, as these two daughters wrote:

> I think the men's stories of abuse by their mothers are very enlightening.

> I get a lot out of hearing the stories of men molested by their mothers. I identify more with them by far than with women molested by their fathers, some of whom unknowingly engage in behavior similar to my mother's (as I also do). At least mother-daughter survivors tend to be more aware of this issue.

The sons answered a similar survey to the one for the daughters, but with modified questions involving genitalia. The survey found that the sons answering the survey were a little older than the daughters; 77% were caucasian; 66% of the sons report their families were working- or middle-class; and 56% were Protestant. Fewer sons than daughters had advanced education, but they made more money than half the daughters. There were also differences in their self-identified sexual orientations (see Table A).

Table A
SEXUAL ORIENTATION OF SONS AND DAUGHTERS ABUSED BY MOTHERS

	Sons	Daughters
Heterosexual	7 (78%)	39 (42%)
Homosexual	1 (1%)	33 (36%)
Bisexual	0 (0%)	9 (10%)
Currently don't know or are uncertain	1 (11%)	9 (10%)
Currently nonsexual	0 (0%)	14 (15%)

Conventional wisdom suggests that men usually find it more threatening than women to indicate they are anything other than heterosexual. Forty-four percent (44%) of the sons are married, and one reports being in a long-term homosexual relationship.

SONS' CHILDHOOD EXPERIENCES

Eighty-nine percent (89%) of the sons believe they had a normal childhood, compared to 2% of the daughters. This major difference may indicate that the sexual abuse was experienced very differently by the sons and daughters. Some possible factors:

First, the sons likely experienced their mothers as true parent figures, indicated by the much lower percentage of sons (33%) than daughters (83%) who reported mother-child role confusion; another third said there was no confusion (compared to 9% of the daughters), and the final third of the sons were unsure (7% daughters). Did the mothers of these sons clearly function more fully as mothers than those of the daughters? Did the mothers more fully abandon their parenting role with daughters when boundaries were crossed? Does society have different expectations of male children that may have had an impact? When asked if there was still mother-child role confusion, 89% of the sons said no (29% of daughters), 11% of the sons said yes (57% of daughters), and none reported feeling unsure (12% of daughters).

Compared to 23% of the daughters, 67% of the sons feel the relationship with their mothers allowed them to achieve adult independence. Despite the abuse, the sons may have received and internalized more nurturance from their mothers.

Second, the sons may have perceptions of the abuse experiences that differ from the daughters' perceptions. One son reported his abuse to be a mix of aggression and seduction, and all the others indicated that they felt like "substitute lovers." One commented:

> I grew up as mother's substitute spouse without overt sexual abuse but felt/recognized mother's interest. I became mature too early without a childhood and have trouble accepting others' attention and love. [There was] no overt sexual contact but verbal attention to my body (sexual jokes) and once found mother in seductive clothing and masturbating during a college years visit. I was a surrogate husband.

Every respondent son believed he had been in a lover-like relationship with his mother. This belief is not true in all cases of mother/son sexual abuse in general, but is a striking finding in this small study. Again, to compare, only 48% of the daughters felt there was any seduction or a lover-like quality in the abuse by their mothers. None (0%) of the sons reported the most violent extreme on a scale of violent to lover-like sexual abuse. However, when asked again but more explicitly, they indicated greater frequency of other abuse, with 44% of the sons reporting accompanying physical abuse (65% of daughters), and 90% of sons reporting accompanying emotional abuse (all of the daughters). In clinical practice I have worked with sons who were quite violently abused by their mothers.

> [It's] just not overt physical violation i.e.: stories, seduction, etc.

> Touching. Not really fondling. Excruciating pain. She pinched the foreskin
> of my penis between 2 fingernails.

Even if a son believed he were his mother's lover, she was still his
mother, and he was her child, as suggested by this son's comment:

> In subtle cases the sexuality may not be obvious, the child may not
> recognize inappropriate responses, and confuse sex with social interactions
> in later years — everything takes on a sexual context. [To address this you'll
> have to] get the client to define/detail situations in non-confrontive or
> labeling ways so clients can comfortably discover [the] inappropriateness of
> [this] behavior before [the] parent is labeled bad and [the] parent-child
> relationship encourages the child to defend/deny facts.

The mothers may have encouraged the sons to see themselves as
lovers, an image that is more socially acceptable than either stereotypical
incest or the homosexual connotations of mother-daughter sexual abuse.
The sons-as-lovers image is also reinforced by social images of male-female
sex. They maintained their belief that they were their mothers' lovers even
where there might have been evidence of other possible motivations —
such as the mother's previous abuse or the lack of other sexual outlets —
for the mothers' behavior.

Two-thirds (67%) of the sons were unsure whether their mothers had
been sexually abused (39% of the daughters were unsure); 11% of the sons
said their mothers had been sexually abused (51% of daughters); none of
the sons thought mom had not been abused (11% of the daughters).

A higher percentage of sons (89%) than daughters (44%) attributed
their mothers' sexual activity with them to a lack of other sexual outlets,
while 11% of sons were unsure (27% of daughters).

Thus, these sons believed they were in a consensual or near consensual sexual relationship with their mothers. They believed (at least in childhood) that they were more sex "partners" than "victims," giving the abuse
a different impact. In a second, more direct question, 44% of the sons said
they believed they were their mothers' lovers.

> Did not realize emotional and sexual abuse until adulthood.

A third factor in the different experiences of sexually abused sons and
daughter may be that the sons were older (average age: 5.7) than the
daughters (average age: 3.2) when the sexual abuse began. These ages represent very different developmental points. The abuse lasted about a year
less for the sons than for the daughters and ended at an average age of 15.

Contrary to reports that mother-son incest may be more damaging than other types, this limited survey suggests that there may have been less disruption of bonding and trust for the sons, less damage to their self esteem, and less interference in their efforts to separate from their families than there was for the daughters.

A fourth factor may be that the socialization of males to be sexually active, aggressive, and heterosexual may protect the sons from some of the emotional problems the daughters experienced.

Still another influencing factor may be that all the sons had spoken to someone about the abuse. Despite that report, 89% of the sons also reported the abuse as the most hidden aspect of their lives. All (100%) of the respondent sons have been in therapy, and 56% of the respondents have told their therapists about the sexual abuse by their mothers. A stunning difference is that only 3% of the daughters reported talking to their therapists. Forty-four percent (44%) of the sons have talked to a spouse or partner, while none (0%) of the daughters have.

The survey asked respondents whether, when they were abused by their mothers, the other parent knew the abuse was happening. Of the sons, 55% said no, the other parent did not know (compared to 27% of the daughters), while none of the sons (0%) thought the other parent knew (20% of the daughters); 33% of the sons were unsure (53% of the daughters). The idea of being sexual with the partner of a grown male must be unnerving for a boy at least sometimes. For their own sense of safety, they may be motivated to believe the other parent (the biological father for 89% of the sons) did not know.

None of the sons told anyone about the abuse during childhood, even though all (100%) report that it was damaging, and 44% of the sons said it was the most damaging experience of their lives.

ABUSIVE ACTS

A final area of difference in the abuse reported by the sons and by the daughters is the actual sexual/physical differences in the abuse by the mothers. Two-thirds (67%) of the sons reported that their mothers fondled their penises, while a third (33%) referred to being fondled on their genitals. Two-thirds of the daughters (69%) were fondled on their genitals.

She presented it as necessary "cleaning."

[She fondled me] while bathing me.

Eleven percent (11%) of the sons were orally stimulated on their genitals by their mothers during the abuse, compared to 25% of the daughters. Twenty-two percent (22%) of the sons experienced their mothers putting fingers inside their rectums, compared to 34% of the daughters (89% of the daughters experienced fingers inside other genital openings).

[She] insisted she apply a medication to [my] rectal opening during youth due to bleeding. [I felt] tension vs. having me apply it myself.

The mothers inserted objects into the rectums of 33% of the sons (51% of the daughters), while none of the sons had objects inserted into their mouths (14% of the daughters). Forty-five percent (45%) of the daughters were abused by their mothers inserting objects into vaginal openings. Enema tubes were the object of choice for the mothers of 44% of the sons, similar to the 45% of daughters sexually abused during enemas. One son added *"Carrots."*

Similar percentages of the sons' and daughters' mothers watched in a way that was experienced as abusive while their children bathed or showered (56% sons, 58% daughters); dressed or undressed (44% sons, 52% daughters); defecated (22% sons, 38% daughters); and masturbated (22% sons, 18% daughters). The mothers of these sons were not interested in or were not observed watching their sons urinate (0%), unlike the mothers of 34% of the daughters. In considering these percentages, keep in mind the vastly disparate sizes of the two samples: this study included ten times as many daughters as sons.

Likewise, similar percentages of sons and daughters were made to watch their mothers expose themselves to them or to others (56% sons, 47% daughters); dress or undress (44% sons, 47% daughters); and masturbate (11% sons, 17% daughters). Nearly the same percentages in both populations were made to bathe with their mothers (22% sons, 20% daughters). Consistently fewer of the sons were made to sleep with their mothers (33% sons, 43% daughters); watch them bathe or shower (11% sons, 38% daughters); or watch them use the toilet (0% sons, 44% daughters). A higher percentage of the sons were made to watch their mothers having sex (22% sons, 15% daughters).

> [I remember her] asking me to wash her back in the tub and [I remember]
> watching her bathe.
>
> ⬚
>
> She would take a sponge bath every day at the same time in the kitchen. It
> does not have to be touching to be abusive. She had me so controlled that
> I would jump over the school wall as soon as the bell rang and race home
> to see her bathe. I would watch her bathe and then go masturbate myself.
> After I masturbated I would feel like shit. Dirty. It would always be
> completed before my dad got home from work an hour later. I have felt
> dirty for most of my life because of this and did not know for sure that it
> was abuse until I talked with my therapist.

The data show a similar pattern of both sons and daughters being made to fondle and touch their mothers (sons: 33% breasts, 22% nipples, clitoris, and vagina, 11% anus and rectum; daughters: 29% breasts, 19% nipples, 25% clitoris, 29% vagina, 3% anus, 4% rectum).

Of the sons, 55% were made to take part in seductive behaviors, activities or games with their mothers (43% daughters) or in ritualized sexualized activities with her (32% daughters). A third of the sons (33%) were made to take part in sexual activities with others while their mothers watched (26% daughters).

The room listed most frequently by the sons as the location of the sexual abuse was the bathroom (89%), followed by the bedroom (67%), the living room (44%), and the kitchen (22%). For the daughters, the bedroom was the most frequent location (75%), followed by the bathroom (58%), the living room (20%), and the kitchen (21%).

CHILD AND ADULT: THE IMPACT OF MOTHERS' ABUSE ON SONS

The impact of the sexual abuse appears different for the sons and daughters. The daughters seemed more frightened and anxious, but the sons were clearly aroused. A higher percentage of the sons (79%) engaged in sexualized behaviors (such as frequent masturbation or peeping) in childhood, compared to daughters (46%); felt sexual excitement (55% sons, 34% daughters); acted out sexually (44% sons, 35% daughters); felt special because of the incest (44% sons, 26% daughters); or sexually abused others (33% sons, 15% daughters). Again, because these percentages represent very different absolute numbers, these comparisons should be viewed with extreme caution.

Another significant difference between the abused sons and daughters is the level of anger and negative feelings reported having been generated in childhood. Significantly lower percentages of the sons reported feelings of depression (56% sons, 69% daughters), anger (22% sons, 50% daughters), rage (22% sons, 52% daughters), and hostility (22% sons, 33% daughters).

> Difficulty in needing to please others, as substitutes for mother, or to gain/maintain "special" status, resulting in my disbelief that I can be liked for my actual self <u>AND</u> have a right to expect others to want/desire to sexually please/satisfy me.

> [I felt] hopelessness, nothing would ever work out/well, numb, life lost its vitality.

Though the sons' negative feelings about the abuse in childhood are important, it is clear that their experiences were different from those of the daughters.

The sons' sleep patterns were reportedly not nearly as often disturbed as those of the daughters. Stress symptoms reported by the sons were generally less severe than for the daughters: only one of the sons (11%) reported any of the listed stress symptoms, specifically migraines, compared to a third of the daughters who experienced migraines. None of the sons reported ulcers (13% daughters), vomiting (18% daughters), headaches (41% daughters), or heart pounding or racing (38% daughters).

The data on negative feelings and stress symptoms may indicate that if a child feels special and believes he or she is a perpetrator's lover, the child may show fewer observable negative signs of sexual abuse initially. However, although the sons indicate less initial stress than respondent daughters, it is clear their abuse was just as damaging. Asked to indicate on a 5-point scale how damaging the sexual abuse by their mothers was, none of the sons said it was not damaging (see Table B). But a higher percentage of sons than daughters felt hopeful about the possibility of recovering from the abuse.

Table B
DAMAGING IMPACT OF MOTHERS' ABUSE

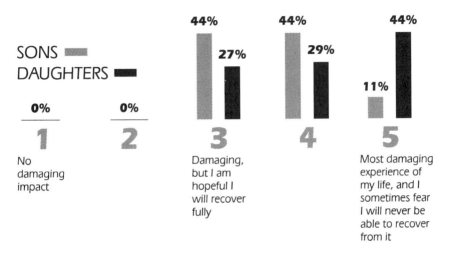

The percentage of sons reporting a sense of being overwhelmed by the abuse rose from 44% in childhood to 78% in adulthood. Although the sons may have "felt special" early in their lives, problems arose later, when they felt decidedly less positive. All of the sons (100%) reported sexual problems in childhood and as adults. Seventy-eight percent (78%) of the sons felt socially isolated in childhood and as adults, while 44% had recurring dreams related to the abuse in childhood and as adults. More of the sons were depressed as adults (78%) than as children (56%); there was more anxiety for the adult sons (89%) than in childhood (56%). And more of the adult sons made suicide attempts (44%) than they did during childhood (33%). Regarding their lives as adults, the sons reported relatively high rates of denial (89%), dependency (89%), self-destructive behaviors (67%), and anxiety attacks (44%).

Law enforcement officials have suggested to me informally that they often find sexual abuse by mothers in the backgrounds of various sex offenders. Specifically they are aware of it among serial rapists and murders. The sons in this study do not report such offenses although several did perpetrate other sexual offenses. A third (33%) said they had sexually abused others in childhood, and 44% have done so as adults; likewise, 33% reported they had sexually abused children after they had become adults (compared to 15% of the daughters in childhood and 3% of the daughters as adults). A third (33%) reported that as adults they had been verbally abusive toward children. The same number of sons (11%) had been physically abusive toward others in their own childhoods and as adults, while 11% also specified they had been physically and emotionally abusive to children as an adult.

> Molested my daughter.

> I sexually abused my daughter. She is [the] primary cause for my treatment. [And] alcohol recovery therapy.

All of the sons (100%) said the sexual abuse by their mothers created problems for them in being parents.

We must not label all male survivors of childhood sexual abuse as potential sex offenders, but it is an important area for future research. If the soaring rate of rape and serial murders is in any way tied to sexual abuse of sons by mothers or other female caretakers, then it is imperative that it be explored fully and quickly.

Sexual identity issues were reported as problematic for 55% of the sons in childhood, decreasing to 33% for the adult sons. In a second question in the survey, 89% of the sons indicated they feel the sexual abuse by their mothers caused them to have "more sexual identity issues than they otherwise would have had." While sexual identity is clearly an issue, at least some of the sons resolve it before or during adulthood.

Sexual confusion can add stress and struggle to a survivor's life. Sixty-seven percent (67%) of the adult sons report feeling "sexually uptight," and 33% report "over-stimulation when sexual" during adulthood. Such conflicts may cause some men to seek low-risk sex in which they feel control or can act out frustration and anger. However, it cannot be assumed that abuse alone would cause abusive or criminal behaviors.

ABUSE-RELATED ISSUES

As did the daughters, the sons reported using drugs and alcohol to numb the pain of their abuse: 67% of the sons report drug or alcohol problems during both childhood and adulthood. Some of the chemical abuse may not stem directly from the abuse, but from the role modeling of the sons' families: 33% of the sons reported that their mothers had an alcohol problem, while 22% reported their mothers' drug problem. "Other parents" of the sons also had alcohol (55%) and drug (11%) problems. It should be noted that more of the sons had a problem with alcohol and drugs than their parents did. One son listed his own diagnosis as "chronic alcoholic."

Thirty-three percent (33%) of the sons report that adult males were in their homes and likely in a relationship with their mothers at the time of the sexual abuse. None reports that the "other parent" was an effective counterbalance to the sexually abusive one. Seventy-seven percent (77%) report this other parent was "hardly ever around" but that 100% of their other parents (fathers) could look normal in public. Only one son said his father was mentally ill.

Eighty-nine percent (89%) of the sons believe the abuse occurred because their mothers had no outlet for their sexual feelings. There may have been impotence among the 55% alcoholic or drug using fathers. Some sons may take on the burden of emotional responsibility for both parents' problems.

RESOLUTION AND RELATIONSHIP

Every son in this study has been in psychotherapy, and two-thirds (67%) feel their abuse-related problems are resolved. This feeling of resolution may represent some denial, given the frequency of depression and sexual problems already mentioned.

> [I feel it's] primarily resolved, but some work still to be done.

Sixty-seven percent (67%) of the sons feel resolved and have forgiven their mothers (compared to 9% of the daughters). Their ability to forgive may be a critical element of their resolution. Resolved or not, 55% of the sons plan on more therapy in the future.

All the sons have been treated in individual therapy, 67% by male therapists, of whom 79% are in private practice. An average of 17 years lapsed between the abuse and first psychotherapy treatment. They've entered therapy an average of 5 times for slightly more than 4 years but some for much longer.

20 years — mostly on, a little off.

❏

Treatment was always a relief and an avenue for possible improvements in my life.

The sons had nearly twice the difficulty of the daughters in maintaining a commitment to continue treatment.

[I] commonly feel discouraged. What's the use? It's not worth it.

More sons than daughters involuntarily entered treatment, but several expressed gratitude for the help. None of the sons report feeling sexually or emotionally abused by a therapist.

It has worked and I'm court ordered to continue it.

❏

It was not hard once I became committed to making the changes in my life I needed to feel free.

Major treatment issues included: trust (66% sons, 94% daughters); the therapist's aggressiveness in addressing issues (66% sons, 50% daughters); dealing with feeling younger than their age (55% sons, 58% daughters); their ability to control the pace of the therapy (44% sons, 50% daughters); dealing with sexual feelings in therapy (44% sons, 61% daughters), and the need to know whether the therapist has had a similar life experience (33% sons, 61% daughters).

Fragmentation of the personality or "splitting" was reported by the sons, with most of the sons (55%) reporting splitting during latency age (ages 5 to 10); a third reported splitting during each of the other age groups (infancy to age 2; pre-school, ages 2–5; and adolescence, ages 11–19). In contrast, most of the daughters experienced splitting during the preschool stage (65%), followed by latency stage (52%), infancy, and adolescence (35% each). This difference may be a reflection of the earlier average age of abuse onset with the daughters (3.2 years) than with the sons (5.7 years). Eighty-nine percent (89%) of the sons also reported they felt stuck or arrested at an early stage of their development.

In adulthood, the sons are 6 times more comfortable than the daughters are in touching their mothers. A larger percentage of sons than daughters have talked to their mothers about their abuse; but like the daughters, they have emotionally and sometimes physically moved away from their mother perpetrators.

All the sons have "created a relationship (real or imagined) which filled mothering function" in their lives. Forty-four percent (44%) of them reported feeling the need to maintain, re-establish, or create a relationship with their mothers, but in a second question, 66% of the sons said they have a desire to withdraw or separate from their mothers.

Fifty-five percent (55%) of the sons have concerns about their mothers' eventual deaths. Others who have experienced their mothers' deaths may be unresolved about her.

She died when I was 22. I felt numb at the time and still do.

This son expresses a fundamental numbness that holds much danger for our society. Given the pain and isolation that virtually all survivors of childhood sexual abuse experience, but especially survivors who hold the last secret of being sexually abused by their mothers, that numbness is the harbinger cloud of a storm of rage on our national horizon. We must encourage the therapeutic release of that electric tension. Already the wind has swept some survivors away; already the lightning has struck in some new lives.

We have to listen to these sons and learn what they can teach us all as they have taught me. As I worked on their data, I was struck by the similarities in the data of the sons and daughters. The sons' data and collective story often seem to "fit" or confirm the data by the daughters. For example, the greatest degree of "splitting" in both the sons and daughters occurs at the ages when the abuse began. When I saw that pattern emerge, I felt gratitude to the sons who responded to the survey, as if they have sung harmony to the daughters' song.

References

Allen, C.M. (1991). *Women and men who sexually abuse children.* Orwell, VT: Safer Society.

American Psychiatric Association. (1994). *Diagnostic and statistical manual of mental disorders* (4th ed.). Washington, DC: Author.

American Psychiatric Association. (1987). *Diagnostic and statistical manual of mental disorders* (3rd ed., revised). Washington, DC: Author.

Bass, E., & Davis, L. (1994). *The courage to heal* (Third Edition). New York: Harper Perennial.

Bear, E. (1993). *Inpatient treatment for adult survivors of sexual abuse: A summary of data from 22 programs.* Brandon, VT: Safer Society.

Bear, E., with Dimock, P. (1988). *Adults molested as children: A survivor's manual for women & men.* Orwell, VT: Safer Society.

Evert, K. & Bijkerk, I. (1987). *When You're Ready.* Rockville, MD: Launch Press

Finkelhor, D. & Associates. (1986). *A sourcebook on child sexual abuse.* Beverly Hills, CA: Sage.

James, B., & Nasjleti, M. (1983). *Treating sexually abused children and their families.* Palo Alto, CA: Consulting Psychologists Press.

Kinsey, A., Pomeroy, W., Martin, C., & Gebhard, P. (1953). *Sexual behavior in the human female.* Philadelphia: W.B. Saunders.

Mathews, R., Matthews, J.K., & Speltz, K. (1989). *Female sexual offenders: An exploratory study.* Orwell, VT: Safer Society.

Nelson, W.E., Behrman, R.E., Kliegman, R. (1990). *Nelson's essentials of pediatrics.* Philadelphia: W.B. Saunders.

Schwartz, M.F. (1991, December). Victim to victimizer. *Professional Counselor,* pp. 43–46.

Usdin, G., Lewis, J. (1979). *Psychiatry in general medical practice.* New York: McGraw-Hill.

Select Safer Society Publications

A Primer on the Complexities of Traumatic Memory of Childhood Sexual Abuse: A Psychobiological Approach by Fay Honey Knopp and Anna Benson (1997). $25.00.

Stop! Just For Kids adapted by Terri Allred and Gary Burns (1997). $15.00.

Female Sexual Abusers: An Exploratory Study by Ruth Mathews, Jane K. Matthews, and Kathleen Speltz (1990). $17.50.

Female Adolescent Sexual Abusers: An Exploratory Study of Mother-Daughter Dynamics with Implications for Treatment by Marcia T. Turner & Tracey N. Turner (1994). $18.00.

Impact: Working with Sexual Abusers edited by Stacey Bird Edmunds (1997). $15.00.

Supervision of the Sex Offender by Georgia Cumming and Maureen Buell (1997). $25.00.

Mother-Son Incest: The Unthinkable Broken Taboo — An Overview of Findings by Hani Miletski (1995). $10.00.

37 to One: Living as an Integrated Multiple by Phoenix J. Hocking (1996). $12.00.

The Brother / Sister Hurt: Recognizing the Effects of Sibling Abuse by Vernon Wiehe, Ph.D. (1996). $10.00.

Men & Anger: Understanding and Managing Your Anger for a Much Better Life by Murray Cullen & Robert E. Freeman-Longo. Revised and updated, new self-esteem chapter! (1996). $15.00.

When Children Abuse: Group Treatment Strategies for Children with Impulse Control Problems by Carolyn Cunningham and Kee MacFarlane. Incorporates and updates their well-respected previous volume **When Children Molest Children,** adding new material on medications, shame and entitlement, firesetting, and animal abuse. (1996). $28.00.

Adult Sex Offender Assessment Packet by Mark Carich & Donya Adkerson (1995). $8.00.

Empathy and Compassionate Action: Issues & Exercises: A Workbook for Clients in Treatment by Robert Freeman-Longo, Laren Bays, & Euan Bear (1995). $12.00.

The Difficult Connection: The Therapeutic Relationship in Sex Offender Treatment by Geral T. Blanchard (1995). $10.00.

Shining Through: Pulling It Together After Sexual Abuse (Second Edition) by Mindy Loiselle & Leslie Bailey Wright (1997). A workbook especially for girls ages 10 through 16. Newly revised and expanded. $12.00.

From Trauma to Understanding: A Guide for Parents of Children with Sexual Behavior Problems by William D. Pithers, Alison S. Gray, Carolyn Cunningham, & Sandy Lane (1993). $5.00.

Adolescent Sexual Offender Assessment Packet by Alison Stickrod Gray & Randy Wallace (1992). $8.00.

The Relapse Prevention Workbook for Youth in Treatment by Charlene Steen (1993). $15.00.

Pathways: A Guided Workbook for Youth Beginning Treatment by Timothy J. Kahn (1990; revised 1992; 3rd printing). $15.00.

Pathways Guide for Parents of Youth Beginning Treatment by Timothy J. Kahn (1990). $7.50.

Man-to-Man, When Your Partner Says NO: Pressured Sex & Date Rape by Scott Allen Johnson (1992). $6.50.

When Your Wife Says No: Forced Sex in Marriage by Fay Honey Knopp (1994). $7.00.

Who Am I & Why Am I in Treatment? A Guided Workbook for Clients in Evaluation and Beginning Treatment by Robert Freeman-Longo & Laren Bays (1988; 7th printing). $12.00.

Why Did I Do It Again? Understanding My Cycle of Problem Behaviors by Laren Bays & Robert Freeman-Longo (1989; 5th printing). $12.00.

How Can I Stop? Breaking My Deviant Cycle by Laren Bays, Robert Freeman-Longo, & Diane Hildebran (1990; 4th printing). $12.00.

Adults Molested As Children: A Survivor's Manual for Women & Men by Euan Bear with Peter Dimock (1988; 4th printing). $12.95.

Family Fallout: A Handbook for Families of Adult Sexual Abuse Survivors by Dorothy Beaulieu Landry, M.Ed. (1991). $12.95.

Embodying Healing: Integrating Bodywork and Psychotherapy in Recovery from Childhood Sexual Abuse by Robert J. Timms, Ph.D., and Patrick Connors, C.M.T. (1992). $15.00.

The Safer Society Press publishes additional books, audiocassetttes, and training videos related to the treatment of sexual abuse.

For a catalog of our complete listings, please check the box on the order form (next page).

Order Form

Date _____

Shipping Address

☐ **Please send a catalog.**

Name and/or Agency _____

Street Address _____
(NO P.O. BOX)
_____

City _____ State _____ Zip _____

Billing Address *(IF DIFFERENT FROM SHIPPING ADDRESS)*

Address _____

City _____ State _____ Zip _____

Purchase Order # _____

Visa or MasterCard # _____ Exp. Date _____

Daytime Phone (_____) _____

QTY	TITLE #	TITLE	UNIT PRICE	TOTAL COST

All orders must be prepaid.	**SUBTOTAL**	
Make checks payable to: SAFER SOCIETY PRESS.	**VT RESIDENTS ADD SALES TAX**	
	SHIPPING *(SEE BELOW)*	
All prices subject to change without notice.	**TOTAL**	

Phone orders accepted with VISA or MasterCard.

NO RETURNS

Mail to:

PO BOX 340 • BRANDON, VERMONT 05733-0340

Phone: (802) 247-3132

Shipping:
- **1–9 items add $5 shipping.**
- **10 or more items add 8% shipping.**
- **Rush Order add $10 and call for actual shipping costs.**

Bulk discounts available:
Please inquire.